IMAGES
of America

THE BENICIA ARSENAL

Louise "Midge" Leavens, a messenger at the arsenal, writes a greeting on a two-ton blockbuster bomb headed for Japan. It reads, "The Voice of Benicia Arsenal to Tokyo." The group of "kibitzers" in the rear are part of the headquarters office. The message was selected by the women because it was a phrase the Japanese could hopefully understand. (Courtesy of the Benicia Historical Museum.)

On the Cover: Taken in 1944 in the tank shop, this photograph shows civilian employees fitting a repaired 75 mm gun to a turret base for an M-4 Sherman tank. The arsenal was equipped to receive back from the theaters of combat any size or type of weapon or ordnance. (Courtesy of the Benicia Historical Museum.)

IMAGES
of America

THE BENICIA ARSENAL

James E. Lessenger and H. Allan Gandy

ARCADIA
PUBLISHING

ISBN 978-1-4671-0963-5

Published by Arcadia Publishing
Charleston, South Carolina

Printed in the United States of America

Library of Congress Control Number: 2022951073

For all general information, please contact Arcadia Publishing:
Telephone 843-853-2070
Fax 843-853-0044
E-mail sales@arcadiapublishing.com
For customer service and orders:
Toll-Free 1-888-313-2665

Visit us on the Internet at www.arcadiapublishing.com

James Lessenger dedicates this book to his grandchildren Quinn and Eve.

Allan Gandy dedicates this book to his wife, Susan.

Contents

ACKNOWLEDGMENTS

This book is a natural product for the Benicia Historical Museum, which for the last 35 years has made its mission to collect artifacts, documents, photographs, personal histories, and articles on the Benicia Arsenal. We have benefited from the work of the late Harry Wassmann (1919–2017), the former executive director of the museum, and the late Josephine Cowell (1897–1986), the official chronicler of the arsenal. Cowell was the public information officer for the arsenal in the 1950s. She wrote histories of the Stockton Depot and the Benicia Arsenal, and her album of photographs, several of them taken herself, forms the backbone of the collection presented in this book. She moved to Utah when the activities of the Benicia Arsenal were transferred to the Toelle Arsenal and retired in 1967.

We are also indebted to the ongoing efforts of Jennifer Roget, the executive director of the museum; Beverly Phelan, curator; and Maureen Williams, office manager. Bob Kvasnicka provided invaluable support with his encyclopedic knowledge of arsenal photographs and the stories behind them. John Halliday, military historian and member of the museum board of directors, helped identify the equipment and weapons in the photos. Special thanks to Randy Potter and Randy Fulk of Unico Mechanical Inc. for allowing us to take photographs of the machine shop.

We are grateful to Jim's wife, Leslie, and Allan's wife, Susan, for their support and editorial advice. Lastly, we thank the editors and staff of Arcadia Publishing for their confidence and aid to get this project to press.

All images used in this book are courtesy of the Benicia Historical Museum unless otherwise noted.

INTRODUCTION

The 117-year history of the Benicia Arsenal is presented in this book in chronological order. While this is a tried-and-true method of presenting a historical narrative, there are important trends that must be explored. In addition, there is a pre-history to the area that became the arsenal. Each of these trends will be examined in this introduction, starting with the pre-history.

Today, the former arsenal is an industrial park of 2,900 acres, full of modern companies of all types. When the Patwin people populated the area before the arrival of the Spaniards, it was rolling grassland scattered with elk, deer, and other wild animals. The Patwin did not establish villages on what is now the arsenal land because of the lack of water, a problem that plagues the arsenal site to this day. They did, however, traverse it between their settled encampments in the Suisun Marsh and the peninsula on the Carquinez Straits that is now downtown Benicia.

The Spanish divided the land into vast grazing ranges and the Mexicans established it as part of Rancho Suscol, a rancho of Mission Solano later owned by Guadalupe Mariano Vallejo (1807–1890). At the dawn of the American period, Robert Semple (1806–1854), California's first journalist, second dentist, and president of the California Constitutional Convention, partnered with Vallejo to establish the City of Benicia, named after Vallejo's wife, Francesca Maria Filipa Benicia Carrillo de Vallejo (1815–1891). As Semple laid out his city, land for a "military reservation" was set aside. He and Vallejo gifted 345 acres to the US Army and the saga of the Benicia Arsenal began.

The size of the reservation was enlarged to fit the mission. The original 345 acres proved to be too small, so the Army methodically purchased property to house more buildings, such as munitions "igloos." By the end of World War II, the arsenal comprised about 2,192 acres. When the base closed, a 700-acre discrepancy along the Carquinez Straits was discovered between the first survey by Lt. William T. Sherman (1820–1891) in 1852 and the final survey done in 1962. The extra land was sediment that had washed down from the hydraulic mining done in the Sierra Nevada mountains during the Gold Rush. Rectifying the difference took multiple meetings and tons of paperwork.

Originally, the first Army forces at the reservation were companies of cavalry, artillery, and infantry occupying wood buildings known as the Benicia Barracks. At the same time, the Benicia Quartermaster Depot was established in wooden warehouses along the straits. Three years later, the Benicia Arsenal was established on land between the two. The three units operated semi-independently, each with a separate mission but sharing infrastructure such as a guardhouse and hospital. After the barracks burned in an explosion and fire in 1922, the three functions were consolidated into the Benicia Arsenal. For simplicity, in this book, the three functions are combined as the Benicia Arsenal.

The weapons evolved. The smooth-bore muskets and cannons of the frontier years gave way to breach-loading weapons with rifling. The cannons became more accurate and with better optics. The vehicles evolved from horse-drawn carts to heavy tanks. Watches, tires, machine guns, shoes, and the like all evolved and required advanced equipment and training. The arsenal entered the space age when Nike missiles arrived.

The missions of the arsenal evolved. The military reservation and barracks were originally erected on the American frontier. California was not yet a state, nor was it a territory. It was a four-year military occupation as Congress debated and dithered about what to do with it. Slavery, of course, was the obstacle. Would there be slavery in California? The arsenal supported cavalry and infantry missions throughout the West. Frontier duty was not only fighting Native Americans, but also doing topographic and engineering studies to learn about this new land. The Army provided dental and medical care to the scattered populations, and it chased banditos.

As the mission of the arsenal evolved, so did the buildings. The original wooden storehouses of the quartermaster depot and barracks of the cavalry post were followed by stone and brick magazines, storehouses, and quarters of the arsenal. Two world wars called for wooden structures of all kinds to be constructed and, in the end, concrete warehouses to house the chemical warfare agents and missiles.

Most important to the function of the arsenal were its people. Combat troops predominated in the initial years as infantry and cavalry units based at the barracks patrolled the West. Along with them came their families and servants. Several officers brought their wives and children. Women did the cooking, kept the homes, and cared for the children. They took in washing and there were "washer women" working at the arsenal. There were slaves in California and Benicia, but there is no evidence that there were any at the arsenal.

In the 20th century, the arsenal army contingent was small, with career officers and non-commissioned officers (NCOs) forming a nucleus that was expanded by civilian workers during times of war, such as World War II and the Korean War.

When the arsenal announced its closing in 1961, other agencies considered the facility for use. One was NASA, which looked at the property for the Manned Space Center. Texas-born vice president and head of NASA Lyndon Johnson was not going to let that happen, and the center went to Houston. One can speculate that if Richard Nixon had won the presidency in 1960, the first words from the moon could have been, "Benicia, Tranquility Base here."

In the end, the arsenal was converted to peacetime uses by a small group of forward-looking citizens in Benicia, Sacramento, and Washington, DC, who saw the chance to create an industrial powerhouse. Mayor James Lemos (1911–1989) and city attorney John Bohm (1909–1983) spearheaded the effort from Benicia, and defense secretary Robert McNamara (1916–2009) and Sen. Clair Engle (1911–1964) organized the effort from Washington. State senator Luther Gibson (1894–1988) and Gov. Edmund "Pat" Brown (1905–1996) organized the efforts in the California government to pass the necessary legislation to make the deal go through. It worked.

One

SELECTION

Manifest Destiny, the campaign cry of the 1844 election, was used by Pres. James K. Polk (1795–1849) to justify the expansion of the United States across North America. He picked a war with Mexico, won it, and incorporated a vast area of land in the Southwest that needed to be patrolled. With the conclusion of the Mexican War in 1846, the Army established a base of operation at the Presidio of San Francisco. From there, they searched the San Francisco Bay area for appropriate locations for logistical bases.

Lt. James A. Hardie (1823–1876) was sent to California in 1846 to help form an army on the Pacific coast. As a temporary major, he joined the 3rd Artillery Regiment, already in San Francisco, where William T. Sherman (1820–1891) was the junior first lieutenant. Hardie took command of all military and civil affairs in the state under the command of Col. Richard Mason (1797–1850), and Sherman became his chief of staff.

Hardie and Sherman selected the Presidio of San Francisco as their administrative headquarters and the military reservation at Benicia as the main logistical base. The site at Benicia was decided upon in 1847 because of its strategic location on the Carquinez Straits that linked the bay to the California interior.

Importantly, the land was free. Dr. Robert Semple, the founder and developer of Benicia, gave the land to the Army to stimulate the sale of real estate lots. Sherman did the first survey of the reservation.

Bvt. Lt. Col. Silas E. Casey (1807–1882) of the 2nd Infantry Regiment became the first commanding officer of the Army outpost when he founded "the post at Point near Benicia" on April 30, 1849. At the same time, the Benicia Quartermaster Depot was established and wooden quarters for both infantry and cavalry units were constructed.

Robert Baylor Semple founded Benicia in 1846. He was also California's first newspaper reporter and publisher, and second dentist. As president of the California Constitutional Convention in 1849, he championed the abolition of slavery. Semple envisioned that giving the initial 345 acres of land to the Army for a military reservation would stimulate the development of Benicia. This photograph was taken during the Constitutional Convention in 1849. Semple typically wore buckskins and a fox-skin cap.

Lt. James A. Hardie, a recent West Point graduate, was sent to California in 1846 to help form the nucleus of an army on the Pacific coast. Hardie was in garrison at the Benicia Arsenal from 1853 to 1858. (Courtesy of Library of Congress.)

In this photograph taken during World War II, the arsenal is in the foreground, and Benicia is behind it. The Carquinez Strait is to the left, and crossing it is the railroad bridge. Pine Lake Reservoir is at center. In the background are the Mare Island Shipyard and the Marin Headlands. Note the submarine barrier to the right of the railroad bridge. The original 345-acre military reservation corresponds to this photograph, with the quartermaster depot to the left, the barracks to the right where the square of trees is, and the arsenal at center.

This 1860s drawing shows the buildings atop Army Point along the Carquinez Strait. This strategic location was an important choke point on the north side of the strait that connects the Sacramento Delta to San Francisco Bay. The Clock Tower warehouse overlooks the straits to the left and the commanding officers' quarters (COQ) are in front of it. The field officers' quarters is at the other end of the parade ground from the COQ. The quartermaster depot is at right, as is the original stone wharf.

Lt. Col. Silas Casey established the Benicia Barracks in April 1849. Casey played a significant role in the military operations in the Pacific Northwest. In addition to maintaining law and order in this Western outpost, he conducted topographical and geographical surveys of the area. He served at the barracks until 1852.

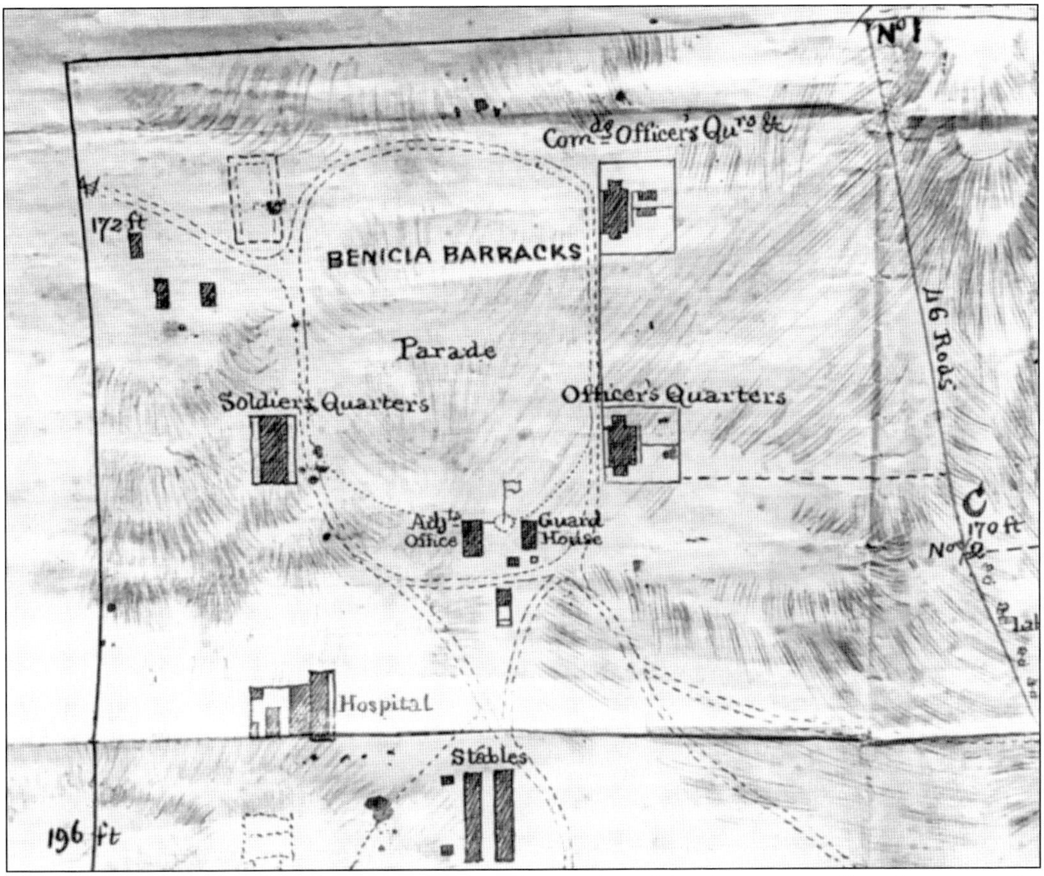

Depicted on this 1856 map of the Benicia Barracks are the soldiers' quarters, officers' quarters, the COQ, an administrative office, a guardhouse with five prison cells, stables, and parade grounds. Dotted lines indicate where future quarters would be built. All the buildings were constructed of wood except the future hospital, which was made from sandstone.

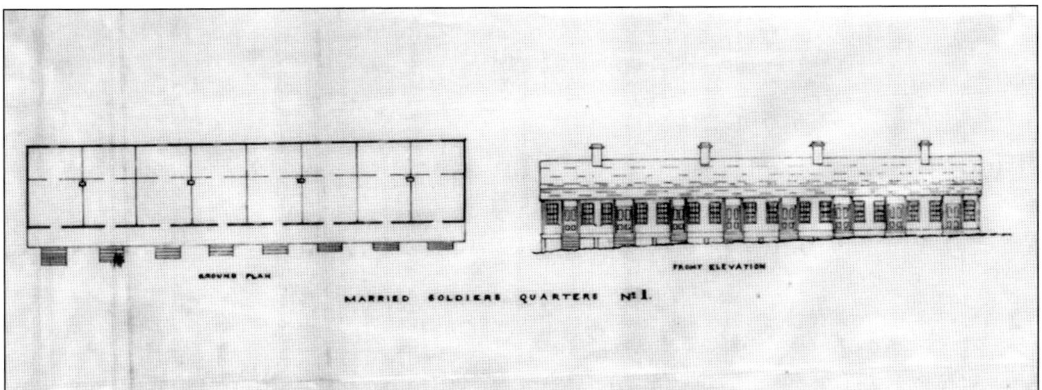

The Army built special quarters for married soldiers. Here is an 1849 drawing of the married soldiers' quarters (Building 1) with eight single-story units. The building was constructed with airspace beneath the floors and a continuous porch. Each unit had two windows and shared a chimney with the adjoining unit.

The Benicia Barracks, established before the ordnance command arrived, built a main gate, and always maintained a soldier on duty. This guard is pictured with his rifle and two young boys, children of soldiers, behind the fence around 1900.

A 30-year-old Lt. Ulysses S. Grant (pictured here during the Civil War) was ordered to California in 1852. He left New York on July 5, crossed the Panama Isthmus, and arrived in Benicia on August 18. He visited Knights Ferry, Vallejo, and Sonoma before departing on September 14 for an assignment in Northern California. He was at the arsenal for 16 days. Contrary to local myth, he was never incarcerated for being intoxicated and never fired a cannonball across the strait. (Courtesy of the Library of Congress.)

Two

Frontier Duty

The infantry barracks, quartermaster depot, and arsenal shared the same reservation but operated semi-independently until 1924, when they were united under one command by Gen. John Pershing (1860–1948).

The Benicia Barracks supported the Modoc Wars, the Pit River Expedition, and the Battle of Battle Mountain (notable because the Native Americans won). Under a separate command, the Benicia Quartermaster Depot was placed along the shoreline of the Carquinez Straits and originally consisted of wooden warehouses, a foundry, and shops. A derelict dismasted ship served as wharf and quarters until a stone T-shaped wharf was constructed into the straits.

The Benicia Arsenal was established on August 19, 1851, by Bvt. Capt. Charles P. Stone (1824–1887). Lacking adequate funding and considering the inferior quality of bricks in California at the time, Stone elected to use local sandstone quarried on the arsenal grounds and redwood transported by ship from the Marin Headlands to construct the buildings. Over the next nine years, a guardhouse, two warehouses, a hospital, five magazines, a wharf, and a fortress-like warehouse were constructed of locally quarried sandstone. One of the reasons for the lack of funding from Washington, Captain Stone discovered, was the concern on the part of the US War Department that the title to the arsenal property was not secure.

The arsenal was part of the Army Ordinance Department's plan for providing weapons and ammunition to the Army. In addition to Benicia, there were arsenals at Watervliet, New York; Allegheny, Pennsylvania; Washington, DC; and St. Louis, Missouri. The Springfield Armory was established during the Revolution to research and manufacture weapons.

Between 1849 and 1944, the arsenal footprint expanded from 345 to 2,345 acres and then shrank through transfers and easements to 2,192 acres. When fully developed, the arsenal consisted of approximately 300 buildings, two motor pools, Nike missile launching and repair facilities, an explosives holding area, and a network of 109 munitions storage igloos.

This photograph, taken during the Civil War, is of Bvt. Capt. Charles Pomeroy Stone (1824–1887), the first commander of the Benicia Arsenal. In January 1851, he issued orders to transfer 21 soldiers (four armorers, five carriage makers, eleven artificers, and one blacksmith) from different arsenals to California to serve under his command. Stone commanded the Benicia Arsenal from 1851 to 1856.

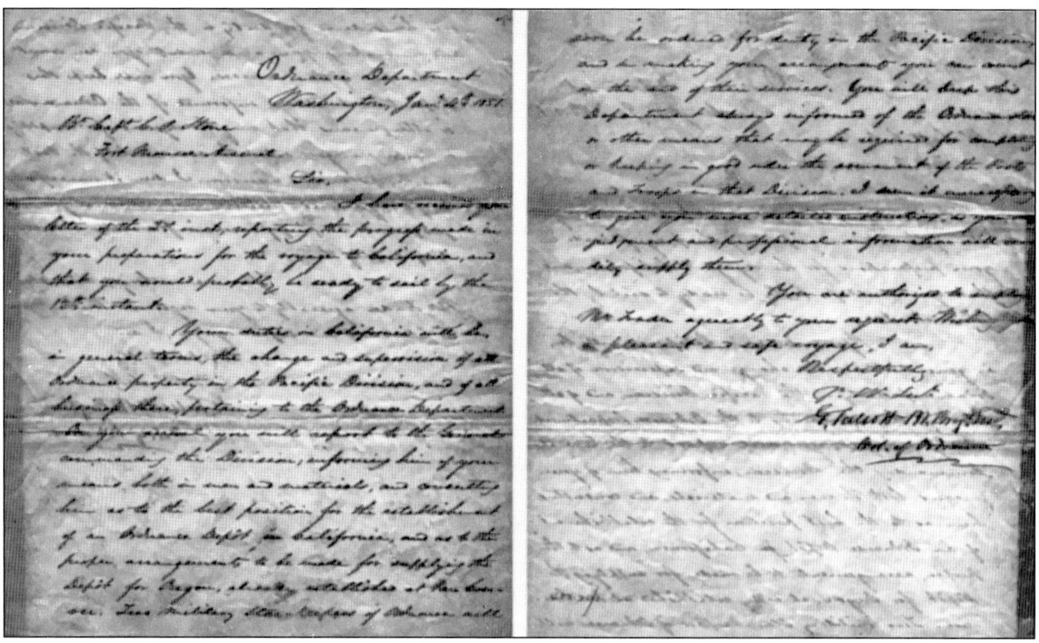

In this letter dated January 4, 1851, from Brig. Gen. George Talcott, commander of ordnance in Washington, DC, to Bvt. Capt. Charles P. Stone, Talcott writes to wish Stone well on his voyage to California. He would be reporting to the commander of the Pacific Division upon arrival to find the best location for an ordnance depot on the West Coast.

This 1877 map of Benicia Military Reserve shows its location along the Carquinez Strait. The legend lists magazines, storehouses, a carpenter shop, a blacksmith shop, soldiers' quarters, officers' quarters, cottages, and laundress quarters.

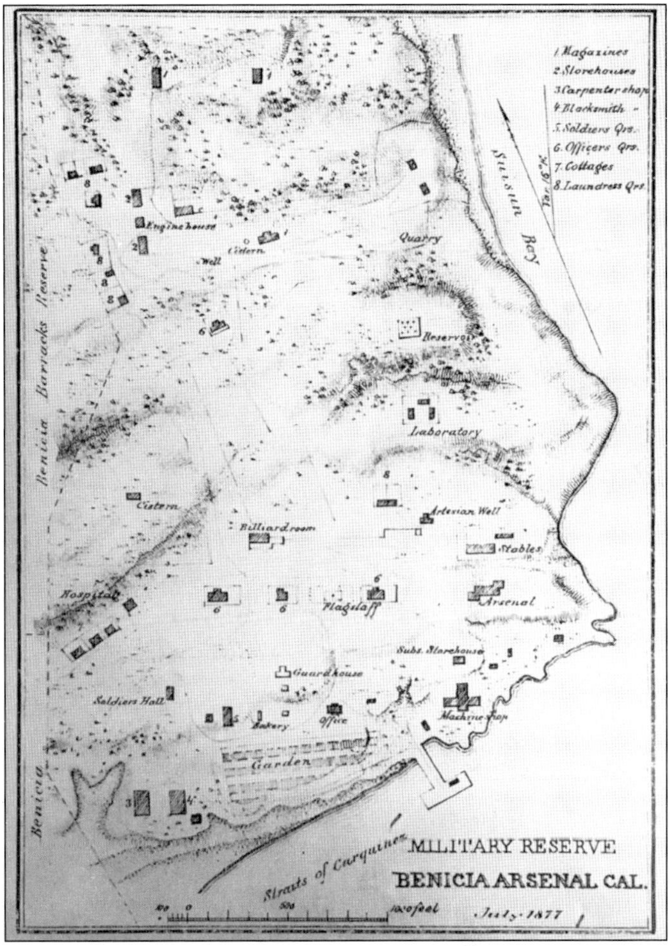

Shown in the 1880s, the main gate was the primary entrance to the Benicia Arsenal. Guards were stationed around the clock with eight-hour shifts. A guard stands at attention near the gate, which has been decorated with cannonballs.

This is a view from inside the main gate looking toward the City of Benicia. The circular structure to the left is an office for the guards. This photograph is from the 1880s; the trees and road are well established.

Here is a modern photograph of Building 7. The two-story storehouse was built in 1853 and was the first of 14 structures built using sandstone from nearby quarries. This building's walls are two feet, six inches thick, and the gabled roof is of corrugated iron. The building measures 40 by 100 feet, and the foundation is stone. It is now used by the Benicia Historical Museum for exhibits and storage.

This World War II–era photograph shows Building 9. Constructed in 1854, this two-story sandstone building is nearly identical to Building 7. The walls are two feet thick and the structure measures 40 feet by 100 feet. Unlike Building 7, the bottom floor is open, with arches down the center.

The lower level of Building 9 is now known as Stone Hall, named after Capt. Charles P. Stone. The floor is made of redwood. The walls were covered in the 1940s with a plaster consisting of lime, sand, and horsehair for use in food service for prisoners of war (POWs).

Built in 1856, the post hospital was the first US military hospital on the Pacific coast and the first purpose-built hospital west of the Mississippi River. Constructed from local Benicia sandstone, the building had a second-story ward, a fireplace at each end, and six offices. After the construction of the new dispensary in the 20th century, it was repurposed as an office for the arsenal chaplain. It is now used as the headquarters of the Port of Benicia.

Shown in this modern photograph, Building 8 is a single-story sandstone building constructed in 1855 and used as a pump house for water that was piped from a spring and stored in a cistern under the floor. The dimensions of the structure are 28 by 35 feet. The walls are two feet thick, the foundation is of stone, and the gabled roof is corrugated iron. Later, the building was used as a guardhouse and a Military Amateur Radio Service station. It is now the office of the Benicia Historical Museum.

Building 2, the first sandstone powder magazine constructed in 1855, is shown in this 1960s photograph. The Army had a contract with master mason Caleb Merrill to build the structure utilizing an Army drawing from 1828. It was constructed of local sandstone with four-foot-thick walls. The interior has six stone columns, wood floors, and wood wall coverings. It could store up to 3,000 barrels of black gunpowder. A fire destroyed the roof in 1983, and the building is unused.

Soldiers in uniform pose at the post hospital in the 1870s. At the time, the medical staff was doing research on communicable diseases.

Building 10 was constructed in 1857 at a cost of $35,262. It is identical to Building 2 except for interior sculptural designs on the columns. Over 90 men, mostly of Irish descent, built the magazine. The master mason was Caleb Merrill. The concrete loading dock was added during World War II.

The most artistic feature of the powder magazine (Building 10) is the eagle and cannon sculpture above the entrance. To the left and right of the cannon is the inscription, "Erected A.D. 1857." The eagle and cannon motif was carved from a single block of sandstone. It is unknown who carved the sculpture, but it was probably mason Peter Larseneur.

This close-up of one of the columns in Building 10 shows an artistic carving. Each octagonal column has four different carvings. There are a total of six columns in the magazine: two with a scroll (pictured), two with pendants, and two with seashells. (Courtesy of the Library of Congress.)

The powder magazine (Building 10) interior includes beautifully carved columns and an arched ceiling. This photograph was taken in 1954. Josephine Cowell, the public information officer for the arsenal, can be seen standing near a column.

When the new arsenal commander, Franklin D. Callender (1817–1882), assumed command in 1856, he requested $50,000 from the Army ordnance office for a new storehouse. The storehouse was constructed from local sandstone in 1859 under the direction of Caleb Merrill, master mason, and Jeramiah Fuss, architect. The clock gave the building the name used today: the Clock Tower. (Courtesy of the Library of Congress.)

Built in 1860, the commanding officers' quarters was one of the most gracious and elegant buildings in California at the time, and quickly became the center of the social life of the post and the surrounding county. The foundations were constructed of cut and dressed sandstone blocks, and the walls were of brick.

The field officers' quarters, a three-story building, was built in 1861. Constructed of brick with two-foot-thick walls, the first level is partially below ground. Today, it is known as the Jefferson Mansion and is used for weddings and special events.

This two-story building was the quartermaster storehouse, built in 1862. Following the Civil War, military material was reconditioned here, including weapons and horse equipment. It sat along the Carquinez Strait and was one of the largest non-sandstone structures built during this time, providing 22,000 square feet of usable space. The building is now gone.

Travelers by boat on the Carquinez Strait saw this view of the 1862 wood storehouse (left) and the stone Clock Tower storehouse (right). The shore along this area was primarily marsh and there were no landing points except for the nearby arsenal wharf. This photograph was taken around 1890.

Pictured here in 1945, the post cemetery is the oldest military cemetery in the Western states. It contains 212 interments dating from 1849 to 1958, including US military personnel, civilians, unknowns, and German and Italian POWs.

This rare image is one of the very few photographs taken just before or during the Civil War and depicts the arsenal buildings in the foreground and the barracks in the background. The powder magazine (Building 10) is in the near foreground.

This photograph taken in the 1920s features officers' row. The COQ is in the foreground and behind it is the officers' quarters. To the right is a greenhouse and in the background are water storage towers. The village of Benicia is in the left background. The parade ground and the tall flagpole are behind the COQ.

Three

The Civil War

In the year before the cannonade fell on Fort Sumter in April 1861 to initiate the Civil War, the arsenal was engaged in an aggressive building program. The brick and stone Italianate commanding officer's quarters, two equally beautiful officers' quarters, and cottages for enlisted personnel were constructed. Additionally, stables, paint shops, a bakery, and other small wooden buildings were constructed.

Julian M. McAllister (1823–1887), then a first lieutenant, was commanding the arsenal at the time. He coordinated with Col. Washington Seawell, commander of the 6th Infantry Regiment at the Benicia Barracks, to protect the magazines and other buildings from Confederate sympathizers.

The factories behind the warehouse, now known as the camel barns, kicked into high gear, and shipped equipment and ammunition to the East Coast. The arsenal shops cleaned, repaired, and manufactured holsters, ammunition boxes and chests, saddles, bridles, and gunpowder. Army troops in all three garrisons (barracks, depot, and arsenal) were transferred to the East Coast.

Filling the void, the Army recruited a force of about 14,000 men designated the California Volunteers (CV). The volunteers consisted of eight regiments of infantry, two regiments of cavalry, a battalion of cavalry, a battalion of veteran infantry, and a battalion of mountaineers. Recruited out of the mines, factories, and fields of California and Oregon, these units were organized by officers who were former Union soldiers. The units formed in their hometowns and then went to the Benicia Arsenal and quartermaster depot to obtain uniforms, equipment, weapons, and ammunition. From there they patrolled the 14 western states to maintain the peace, subdue Confederate sympathizers, especially in Visalia and Wilmington, California, and keep the northern trade and communication routes open. The arsenal also supplied militia units such as the Benicia Rifles and the Petaluma Guards. The initials "CV" were placed after the names of regiments in the California Volunteers to distinguish them from regiments with the same numerical designation in the regular Army fighting on the East Coast. The arsenal also supplied similar volunteer forces in Oregon and Nevada.

In 1864, the Army transferred 38 camels from the Drum Barracks in Wilmington to the arsenal to be sold at auction. The "Camel Experiment" brought camels from the Middle East to the Pacific Southwest to test whether they could be adapted to Army use patrolling the vast deserts. The Camel Dragoons were disbanded, and the remaining camels were sold. While in Benicia, the camels were housed in corrals behind the storehouses (Buildings 7, 8, and 9).

Pictured here are soldiers of Company E, First Infantry Regiment, CV. Notably, they were stationed at the barracks during the Civil War.

Seen here are two soldiers from the 3rd Infantry Regiment, CV, during the Civil War. This regiment was organized at Stockton to serve three years and was at the Benicia Barracks from September 15 to December 3, 1861.

This document contains the final guilty verdict issued for Pvt. Peter Kleinkopf, Company E, 4th Infantry, CV, on charges of desertion, assault with intent to commit robbery, and assault with intent to commit murder. Kleinkopf was executed during the summer of 1863 by a firing squad at the Benicia Barracks, the only execution to occur in the West during the Civil War. (Courtesy of the National Archives.)

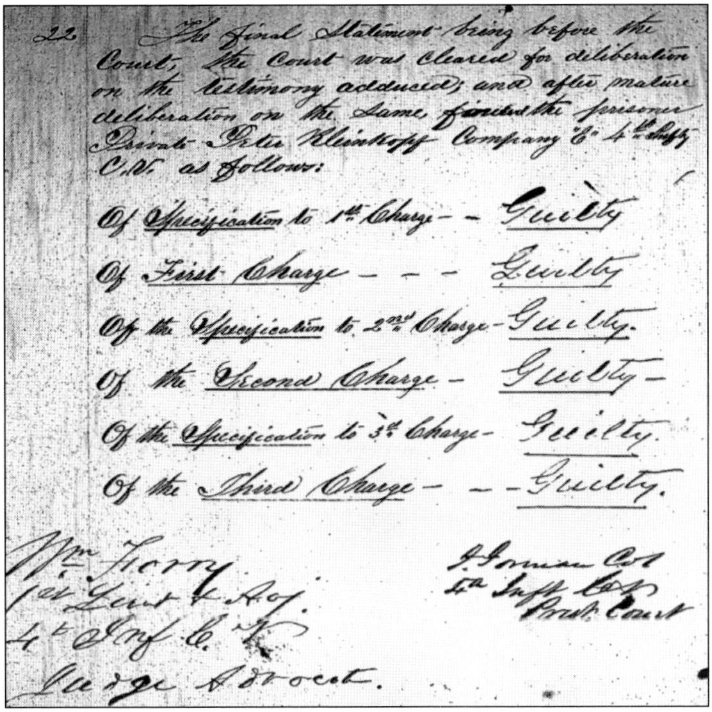

22 The Final Statement being before the Court, the Court was cleared for deliberation on the testimony adduced; and after mature deliberation on the same, finds the prisoner Private Peter Kleinkopf Company "E" 4th Infy C.V. as follows:

Of Specification to 1st Charge - - Guilty

Of First Charge - - - Guilty

Of the Specification to 2nd Charge - Guilty.

Of the Second Charge - Guilty -

Of the Specification to 3rd Charge - Guilty.

Of the Third Charge - - - Guilty.

Wm. Ferry
1st Lieut & Adj.
4th Inf C.V.
Judge Advocate.

J. Forman Col
4th Infy C.V.
Prest. Court

This is the first guardhouse at the Benicia Military Reservation built in 1851 and located in the Benicia Barracks complex, pictured around 1890. It was a wooden building measuring 26 by 50 feet and contained a general prisoner area, five prisoner cells, and a guard area. This was where Private Kleinkopf was detained before his execution in 1863. (Courtesy of the Library of Congress.)

From left to right, Buildings 9, 8, and 7 are viewed from the back in this photograph taken in the early 20th century. In the 1860s, the Army experimented with using camels as pack animals in the Southwest. When the project was abandoned in 1864, a total of 38 camels were brought to the arsenal for auction. The camels were stabled in corrals behind Building 9. The soldiers,

seeing camels around the barn-like buildings, nicknamed the structures "Camel Barns," a name still used today. These buildings are now the home of the Benicia Historical Museum. (Courtesy of the Library of Congress.)

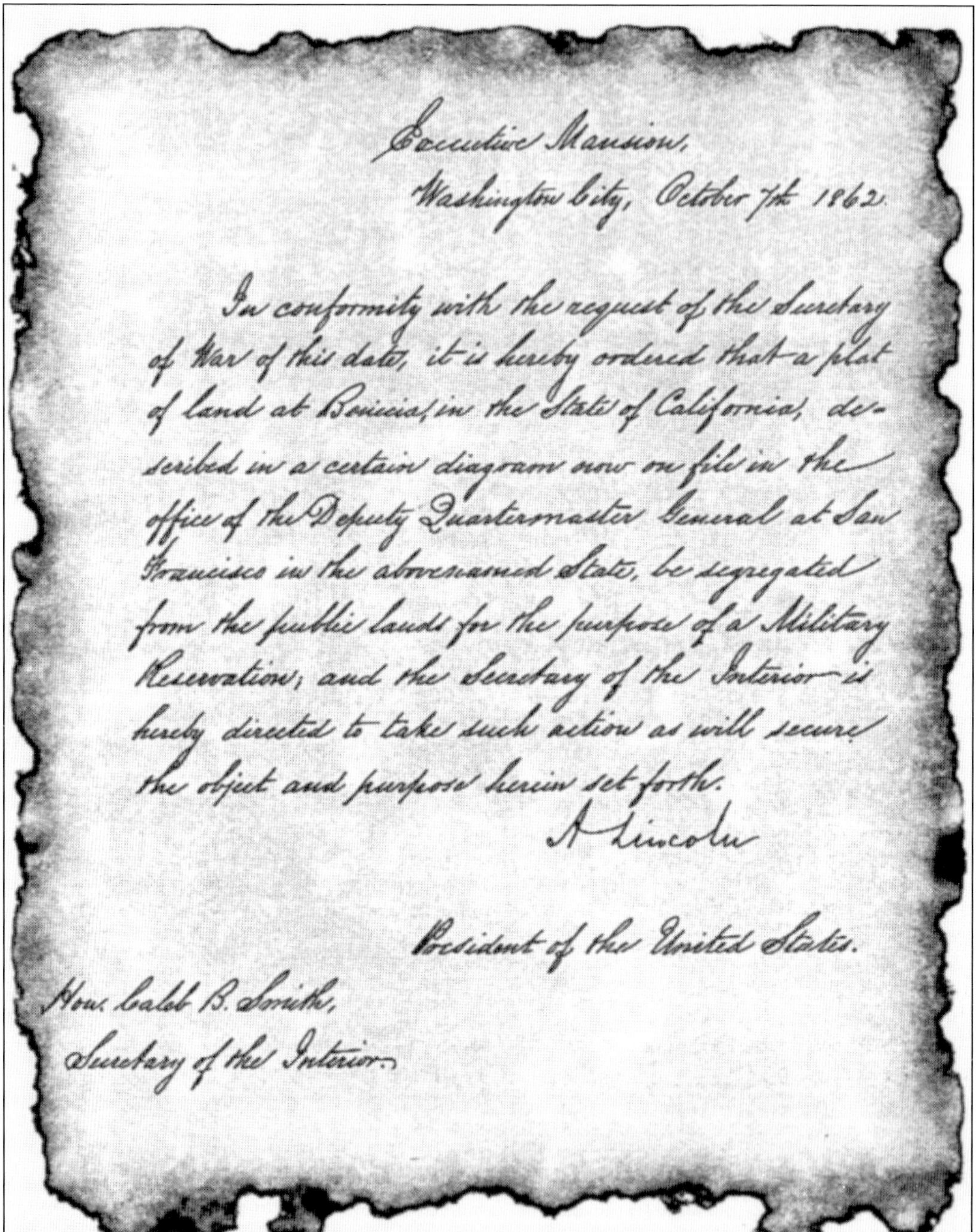

Executive Mansion,
Washington City, October 7th 1862.

In conformity with the request of the Secretary of War of this date, it is hereby ordered that a plat of land at Benicia, in the State of California, described in a certain diagram now on file in the office of the Deputy Quartermaster General at San Francisco in the abovenamed State, be segregated from the public lands for the purpose of a Military Reservation; and the Secretary of the Interior is hereby directed to take such action as will secure the object and purpose herein set forth.

A Lincoln

President of the United States.

Hon. Caleb B. Smith,
Secretary of the Interior.

This executive order signed by Pres. Abraham Lincoln on October 7, 1862, required that public lands at Benicia be segregated for the purpose of a military reservation. It was signed by Lincoln and the secretary of the interior, Caleb B. Smith. This order became necessary when the Rancho Suscol decision by the Supreme Court in 1862 invalidated all previous land claims in the area, including the Army's 1849 deeds to the land. (Courtesy of the National Archives.)

Four

Serving the Pacific Rim

The period between the Civil War and World War I was a time of intense domestic and foreign military activity. The United States expanded into the Pacific regions, and new types of weapons, munitions, and equipment were introduced to the Army inventory while old types were withdrawn and scrapped.

The domestic missions of the Benicia reservation included patrolling the vast southwestern United States. The Army was engaged in simultaneously suppressing and protecting different Native American populations and protecting European populations. Topographic expeditions were launched to document ports and routes for railroads. The Army also provided protection to railroad construction crews from Native Americans and bandits. Veterinary and medical activities were centered at the arsenal, including food safety.

The United States entered the international theater on the Pacific Rim after the Civil War. The arsenal provided weapons, supplies, and ammunition to forces in Hawaii, the Pacific, and the Far East. It equipped forces for the Philippine-American War of 1899, the Spanish American War of 1899, the Philippine occupation of 1899 to 1946, the Boxer Rebellion in China of 1899, and the Russian Revolution of 1917.

The nature of warfare and the weapons changed. Breech-loading rifles and cannons replaced muzzle-loading weapons. Automobiles replaced the horse and carriage. The Army constructed large defensive positions on the San Francisco peninsula, the Marin highlands, Hawaii, the Philippines, and Oregon. All these locations were supplied from the arsenal. The weapons included 16-inch cannons that required vast tonnages of gunpowder manufactured in a special laboratory on the arsenal grounds. To deliver these new materials, the arsenal embarked upon an aggressive building program.

Col. Julian McAllister (1823–1887) was the commanding officer of the arsenal from 1860 to 1886 and built many of the buildings. He participated in Benicia's social life and was instrumental in the planning and construction of St. Paul's Episcopal Church. During these years, the arsenal was the social and cultural center of Benicia.

From 1868 to 1884, the Army built the officers' quarters, soldiers' barracks, command post, guardhouse, and shops. Pictured is a non-commissioned officers' quarters (Building 24) constructed in 1868 at a cost of $8,164. It is a wood frame structure with composition shingles and two stories measuring 43 feet by 25 feet. On the first floor were a sitting room, dining room, kitchen, pantry, and bathroom. The second floor contained two bedrooms. It is still in use as a residence.

Pictured during World War II, this family officer's quarters (Building 33) was constructed in 1870 at a cost of $1,600. It measured 39 feet by 51 feet and had a wooden structure and floors. On the first floor were a sitting room, den, dining room, kitchen, sewing room, and bathroom. The small second floor contained two bedrooms. It is still in use as a residence.

Seen during World War II, this non-commissioned officers' quarters (Building 35) was erected in 1870 at a cost of $1,600 and was 1,800 square feet. The name of the current officer was listed on the top step of the stairs. Over the years, this building was home to Technical Expert Sgt. S.S. Clement, WO G.L King, and WO M. O'Donnell. It is still in use as a residence.

This photograph taken in the 1890s shows a two-story wood building. Built in 1870, it served as an office for the post quartermaster.

Photographed during World War II, the Command Post (Building 47) on Grant Street was built in 1870. The structure was 2,600 square feet, with thick walls and wood floors. There were masonry vaults and a central heating system running from the two chimneys. It is used today for professional offices.

The guard and engine house (Building 39) seen here before World War II is an exceptionally good example of 19th-century military architecture. It coupled two distinct functions into a compact structure by placing the guardhouse in front of a larger fire engine room. It was built in 1872 at a cost of $11,725. Today, it is a privately owned meeting venue on Adams Street.

Taken during World War II, this photograph shows the back side of the guardhouse and engine house, with a 1937 GMC fire engine with a front-mounted pump on the ramp. The dimensions of the engine house are 48 feet by 24 feet. It has door openings measuring 10 feet by 10 feet and a ceiling height of 15 feet, 10 inches. The engine house could house two fire engines.

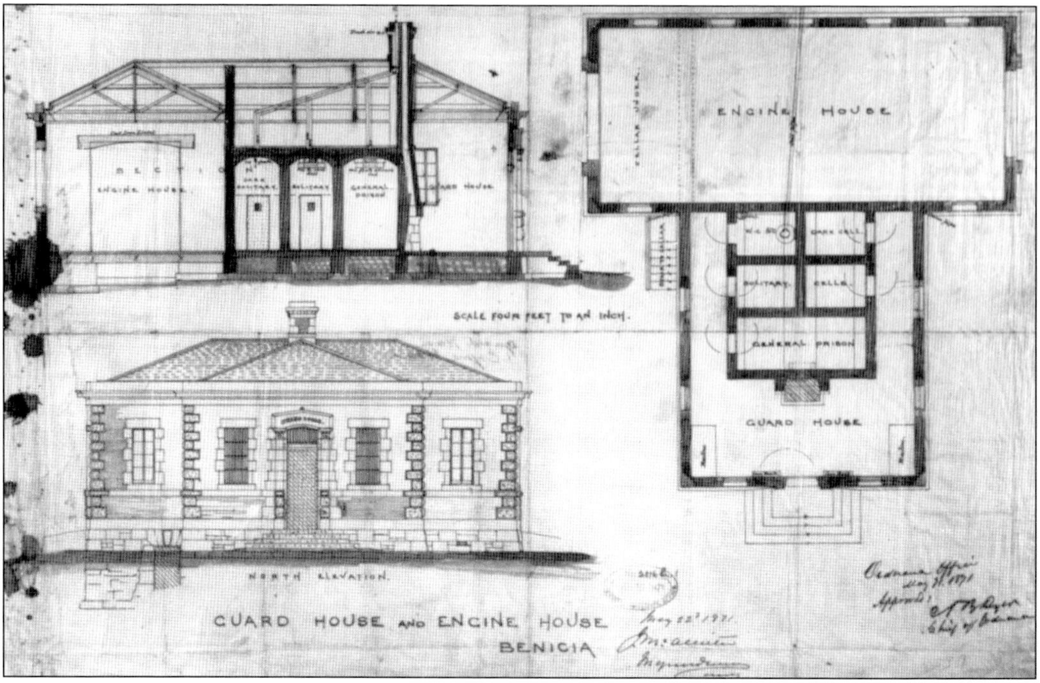

These are the 1871 plans for the guard and engine house. The front of the building contained an office, a fireplace, and quarters for the guard. The center area contained a central prison area, two solitary cells (five feet by seven feet), a dark cell (five feet by seven feet), and a water closet.

The officers' duplex (Building 25–26) was built in 1874. The structure was built as a double house, with two entrances and two hallways. Each half contained a parlor, sitting room, kitchen, pantry, and laundry room on the ground level. Upstairs, there were bedrooms and bathrooms. It is privately owned today and is used as apartments. The photograph was taken in the 1890s. (Courtesy of the Library of Congress.)

From left to right, the blacksmith shop (Building 55) was built in 1876, the machine and optical shop (Building 57) followed in 1884, and then the carpenter and small arms shop (Building 56) was erected in 1877. These buildings are in the lower arsenal area and contain large interior open spaces covered by three different roof truss systems. They are used today for light manufacturing, including a vintage wallpaper company. (Courtesy of the Library of Congress.)

The arsenal blacksmith crew is posing in front of the newly constructed blacksmith shop in 1910. One man is sitting in an early automobile. Automobiles were scarce in the arsenal and were mostly used by officers and shop supervisors.

The US Army Ordnance Board decided in 1880 that muzzle-loading cannons must be retired from the field. The complete conversion to breech-loading artillery took place between 1881 and 1905. Excess cannonballs at the arsenal were stored behind Building 7 and other out-of-the-way locations, as seen here around 1890.

The Central Pacific Railroad Co. completed construction of the rail route between Benicia and Suisun in December 1879, when this photograph was taken. This route to Benicia passed below the Clock Tower warehouse along the Carquinez Strait shore to the Solano Ferry slip at the end of First Street.

The Army Point railroad stop was built in 1880 and served all three functions of the military reservation. This photograph was taken in the 1890s.

Soldiers are mustering in line with combat dress and rifles on the parade grounds in 1897, waiting for an inspection. The parade grounds were located at the time between the commanding officers' quarters and the bachelor officers' quarters.

Two soldiers pose with cannons and cannonballs in about 1898. The two different cannons pictured here are short-barreled and long-barreled howitzers. This photograph is of a test range, designed to test gunpowder for velocity, range, and pressure. The Army was making a transition to smokeless powder, called "brown prismatic powder."

This photograph captures the view from the commanding officers' quarters of the garden and reflecting pool, facing east toward the Clock Tower warehouse. This photograph was taken by Frank J. Stumm, a jeweler in Benicia who was permitted to take pictures in the arsenal and made them into postcards in the early 1900s. The towers contained a mechanism for manufacturing lead musket balls.

Lt. Col. James Walker Benét (1857–1928) was chief ordnance officer at the arsenal from 1905 to 1911. He married Frances Rose of Philadelphia in 1883 and is the father of Stephen Vincent Benét, poet and author.

Stephen Vincent Benét (1898–1943) was an American poet, short-story writer, and novelist. Benét was successful in different literary forms, including novels, short stories, screenplays, and radio broadcasts. He lived for a short time in the COQ when his father was the commanding officer of the arsenal. His most famous work is the book-length poem of the Civil War, *John Brown's Body*, for which he received the Pulitzer Prize in 1929.

A crowd of spectators is seen watching a baseball game in a field with the barracks in the background. This game was played around 1900 between teams from different Army departments. Outdoor activities, such as sports and tug-of-war, were essential to the morale of the soldiers.

On October 18, 1912, a fire and explosion destroyed the main storehouse (the Clock Tower) at the arsenal. The fire consumed 35,000 rifles, 15 million rounds of ball cartridges for small arms and Gatling guns, and equipment for 30,000 soldiers. The explosion rained debris over the military reservation and city of Benicia. The cause of the fire was believed to have been the spontaneous combustion of the ammunition on the second floor.

After the fire of 1912, the interior of the Clock Tower building was in shambles. Fluted iron columns that supported the second floor can be seen bent and twisted by the heat. The other debris consisted of sandstone, melted guns and rifles, artillery shell fragments, and roofing materials. (Courtesy of the Library of Congress.)

The Clock Tower is shown during World War II after rebuilding with two stories and one tower. Reconstruction took about three years, as debris removal, redesign, and rebuilding were difficult. The damaged clock was not replaced until years later. The concrete structure to the right was a bomb shelter and is still in place. After the war, the building was used as a National Guard armory and is today an event venue. (Courtesy of the Library of Congress.)

Men are seen loading 114-pound powder sacks for "Big Gun" 12-inch rifles in about 1900. These cartridges were made for Battery Kirby, an Army defense location north of the Golden Gate Strait in Marin at the entrance to the San Francisco Bay. These 12-inch guns had a range of 10,000 yards (5.7 miles). The factory was probably in Building 7 or 9.

Taken around 1904, this photograph shows the medical staff out for a joyride in front of the hospital. Notice the driver is wearing a mask and goggles. This automobile is a 1903 Pierce Arrow, modified and painted for the Army Signal Corps. It may have been the first Army automobile on the West Coast.

Five

World War I

By the onset of the first world war on April 6, 1917, the arsenal had expanded its facilities to include compressed air hammer operations, modern machine tools, and graded and macadamized roads to replace the dirt surfaces.

During the war, the civilian personnel strength increased from 45 people to a peak of 300 workers. The arsenal supplied equipment for the mobilization of new camps on the West Coast. Arsenal shops serviced all the weapons for the 91st Division before it shipped out to Europe. The facility continued to supply Army installations on the West Coast, Hawaii, and the Philippines.

As in previous conflicts, equipment and supplies were returned to the arsenal after the armistice for repair, storage, or scrapping. This included weapons of all calibers, vehicles, and other materials of war.

Soldiers of a California regiment are seen sitting on the steps of a barracks building around 1915. With the start of World War I, the arsenal and quartermaster depot supplied the permanent Army posts on the Pacific coast, the mobilization of Camps Lewis, Kearny, and Fremont, and the 91st Division's weaponry before it sailed for France.

This Fourth of July parade on Benicia's First Street in about 1917 included arsenal soldiers marching, followed by an automobile with a large US flag. The streets were still dirt, but the sidewalks now had wooden planks.

On draft registration day, June 5, 1917, Benicia businesses, plants, and saloons were closed for the big event. A gathering on First Street is shown. Of the 318 men aged 18–21 who registered, 99 were aliens, 83 had dependent relatives, 36 claimed occupational exceptions, and 2 were disabled, which left 98 eligible for the draft.

In December 1906, the Army put out a general order requiring disc-shaped ID tags (called "dog tags") to be worn by all soldiers. The 1.375-inch aluminum tags were stamped with a soldier's name, rank, company, and regiment or corps, and were attached to a cord or chain that went around the neck. Pictured are dog tags worn by soldier Richard Foley, service No. 1428359. Foley lived in Benicia and was stationed at Camp Cody in Deming, New Mexico, in 1917.

World War I soldiers are seen on the steps of the brick barracks (Building 45) in about 1918. This building was erected in 1872 and expanded in 1919. There are three levels: the basement (storeroom, furnace, and shower-bath), the first floor (day room, dining room, kitchen, and barbershop), and the second floor (sleeping quarters). There were a set of stairs inside on each side of the structure. The building was later enlarged with an extension to the left and is now used as private apartments. (Courtesy of the Library of Congress.)

This c. 1918 photograph shows the inside of the barracks (Building 45) on the first-floor level. The area was used as sleeping quarters with bunks, tables, chairs, and guns in a rack. This level had immediate access to the front porch and stairs to the outside.

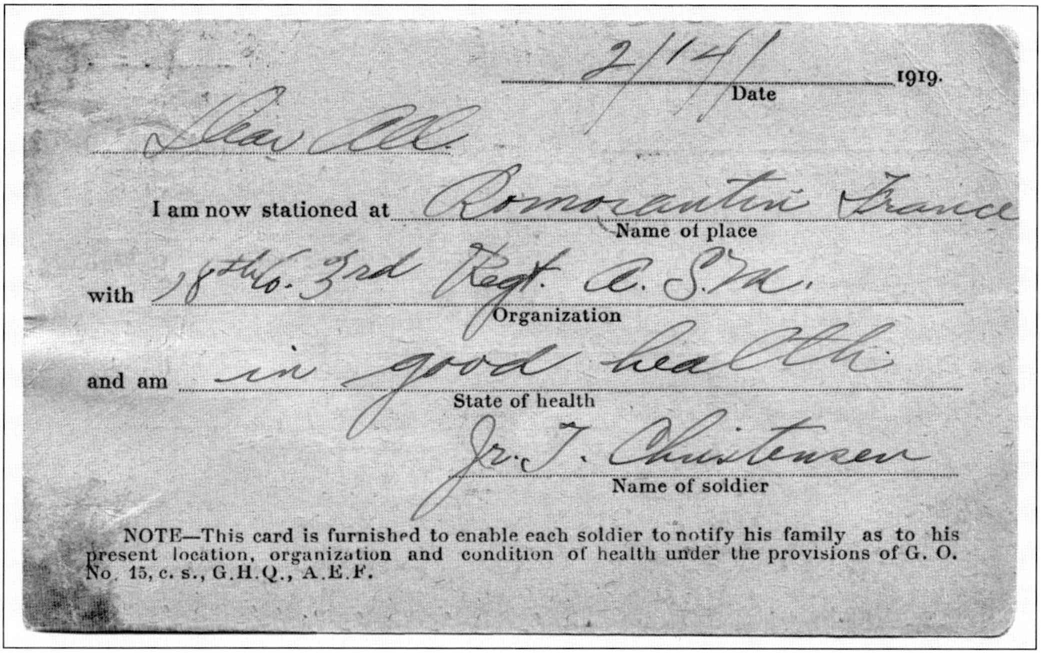

2/14/ 1919.
Date

Dear All

I am now stationed at Romorantin France
Name of place

with 18th Co. 3rd Regt. A.S.M.
Organization

and am in good health
State of health

Jr. T. Christensen
Name of soldier

NOTE—This card is furnished to enable each soldier to notify his family as to his present location, organization and condition of health under the provisions of G. O. No. 15, c. s., G.H.Q., A.E.F.

The World War I location card was a postcard used by soldiers to notify their families of where they were stationed. This card is from T. Christensen Jr., who was stationed at Romorantin, France, with the 18th Company, 3rd Regiment, Air Service Mechanics. The card, which required no postage, was sent to Christensen's wife, A.J., in Benicia.

Besides drills, the Army included outdoor activities to keep up the conditioning and morale of the soldiers. Shown here is a tug-of-war exercise in a field with the barracks in the background around 1915. The soldiers are wearing fatigue uniforms for this activity.

Col. Herman Walter Schull (1875–1968), pictured here while at West Point, was the commanding officer at the arsenal at the start of World War I. He became acting chief of the Inspection Division, Ordnance Department. In 1918, he was awarded the Army Distinguished Service Medal for exceptionally meritorious and distinguished services.

An Army official stands next to a Mark VIII American Liberty Tank in the arsenal in 1919. This tank is one of 100 built in 1918 as an improvement to previous tanks in case World War I lingered on. The design of this tank was unique as it located the engine in the rear and had a sound wall protecting the eight-man crew from excessive noise.

Six

Between the Wars

The period between World Wars I and II was a time of momentous change. The civilian workforce shrank again, and the Clock Tower storehouse was reconstructed. There were changes in the weapons used by the Army, which necessitated the salvage of old ammunition and equipment.

On August 12, 1922, a spark generated from a three-inch shrapnel round being disassembled by a worker at a plant in the Benicia Barracks area caused loose grains of black powder to ignite on the ground. The fire spread rapidly and soon spread to buildings. A magazine, half of the soldiers' quarters, and other buildings were destroyed, at an estimated loss of $375,000. Explosions left permanent divots in the camel barns.

In 1924, the barracks, arsenal, and quartermaster depot, covering 345 acres, were officially combined by order of Gen. John N. Pershing, who personally came to Benicia to officiate at the ceremony that solidified the order.

A massive construction program was initiated in the 1930s. A new concrete wharf, costing $3,416,144 and capable of docking four ocean-going transports, was constructed. A total of 109 igloo-type concrete bunkers were built in the hills around the arsenal for the storage of ammunition. An attractive new headquarters building was erected in the Spanish Revival style, featuring a beautiful cast concrete entrance and interior tiles. Also constructed was a shop building to refurbish artillery and combat vehicles, warehouses, utility and office buildings, and various lesser structures. Roads were constructed or realigned. The electrical, water, and telephone systems were reconstructed and expanded. The sewers were extended, but the arsenal continued to dump raw sewage into the Carquinez Strait until the City of Benicia constructed a sewage treatment plant in the 1960s.

This soldier is standing in front of the Clock Tower storehouse dressed in his World War I–era uniform around 1920. The building was reconstructed after the fire of 1912 as a two-story storehouse with only one tower. It still had the capacity to supply military equipment to the West Coast and Pacific Rim.

The new Spanish Revival headquarters building erected in 1941 had three floors and 59 offices. The building, located on Hayes Street, is now home to a software company, an attorney, an accountant, consultants, contractors, and a miniatures club. The ornate entrance is constructed of cast concrete using Spanish Colonial designs.

On January 24, 1920, General of the Armies John J. Pershing (1860–1948) arrived in Benicia for an inspection on a cold and foggy day. An estimated 10,000 people came to get a glimpse of the greatest military figure of his time. Pictured is General Pershing and arsenal commander Col. Phillip O'Hern (1872–1945) as he inspects the troops.

On August 13, 1922, fifteen employees of the Columbia Salvage Company of New York contracted by the Army were working at Building 11, the magazine pictured in the distance of this photograph, approximately 700 feet north of the camel barns (Building 7). The magazine was ground zero for a fire that started as workers were salvaging brass shells by removing the gunpowder.

The aftermath of the 1922 fire and explosion shows a devastated area where Building 11 once stood. The fire spread to the arsenal grounds on the northern side. Bricks, shells, and other debris can be seen scattered around the area, with a soldier in the background. Pieces of debris from the explosion rained down on the surrounding area, including the village of Benicia. As part of the cleanup, eight tons of unexploded French grenades were buried in a pit near Building 7. In 2005, a massive cleanup program by the Army Corps of Engineers removed the still-live grenades and disarmed them.

An officer poses with a shell found in the remains of the devastated barracks, officers' housing, and Building 11. All the buildings that comprised the original Benicia Barracks were damaged beyond repair or destroyed. The projectile is from a 105 mm howitzer shell. The fire occurred in the heat of August among a field of dry grassland, trees, and wooden structures, so it spread quickly and affected a large area. There were no deaths or injuries recorded.

This image shows the arsenal shops around 1940. The facility had not yet been laced with railroad tracks, and the tidelands to the right were not yet been filled to use for processing tracked vehicles.

A soldier sits in the burned-out remains of a four-chambered cistern destroyed in the fire and explosion of 1922. In 1926, the brick shell of this cistern was reconditioned for use as a magazine, designated as Building 12, and used for storage of chemical warfare agents such as mustard gas. This building was later covered with grading fill in the 1960s when Caltrans constructed the approaches to the Benicia bridge.

Rudolph "Rudy" Quandt is pictured in 1922 driving a LaFrance fire truck. American LaFrance was (and still is) an American vehicle manufacturer focused primarily on the production of fire engines. Rudy was posted at the barracks during World War I and later became a first sergeant in the 1940s.

The Army provided several types of vocational training for enlisted soldiers at the arsenal. Pictured here in 1920 are soldiers being trained on steam roller operation to support the construction and repair of the arsenal roads. Other vocational instruction included automobile driving and tank operation.

The Army was constantly in search of water. Test wells were drilled all over the reservation, but only one, near the COQ, came in without sulfur contamination. One project was abandoned after a well drilled to 1,407 feet did not reach water. In 1939, a project was started to build a 47-foot-high dam at a natural sulfurous spring on arsenal grounds. The Pine Lake Reservoir, shown here, was created with a capacity of 86 million gallons.

Pine Lake Reservoir drafted water from the annual spring runoff of the Carquinez Strait in 1939. Never intended as a source of potable water, Pine Lake was used only as flood control to protect a reservoir downstream, for irrigation water, and to provide water for firefighting.

Pine Lake is pictured in this aerial view from the early 1960s. After the arsenal closed, legal battles over the control and safety of the reservoir between different agencies resulted. Pine Lake was filled in with gravel in 1988 so it could no longer retain water and function as a reservoir, removing the state regulators from control.

Constructed in 1942, the wharf, shown here in 1944, could accommodate up to four 10,000-ton sea-going cargo ships. The wharf was equipped with truck and rail service and a 60-ton-capacity floating crane. It was located along the Carquinez Strait just south of the Clock Tower. The wharf is still in use and now receives vehicles from all over the world brought to Benicia for processing. It also is used to ship petroleum coke, a byproduct of the Benicia refinery.

A total of 109 igloo-type concrete bunkers were constructed between 1939 and 1941 in the hills around the arsenal for underground storage of ammunition and other sensitive materials. The bunkers provided protection from outside intruders as well as camouflage from aerial attacks.

The interior of an igloo bunker reveals stored pallets of howitzer shells. Unvented apart from a top vent to keep the ammunition dry, the bunker is concrete construction and 25 feet wide, 15 feet high, and 40 feet deep. It has 874 usable square feet and was built at a cost of $3,900. The bunkers are now used for storage, and several have been incorporated into an asphalt plant. One bunker is used by the museum to store Christmas decorations.

The arsenal staff pose in front of the new administration headquarters in 1941 before the United States entered World War II. The building was equipped with the latest communication equipment, including telephones, telegraphs, and teleprinters. This group was key in keeping the Army up to date with current information.

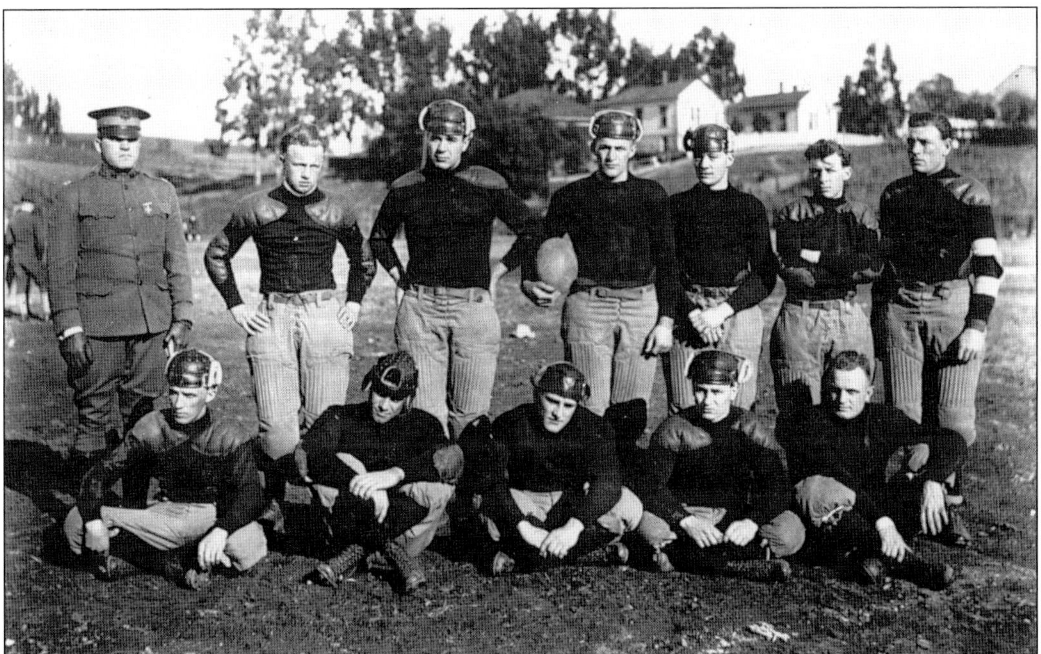

The Signal Corps football team is shown here in the 1930s. Sports were and continue to be important to the Army for fitness and team building. Importantly, they also keep the troops occupied.

Built in the early 1940s, the arsenal dispensary was equipped and staffed to give first aid and execute the industrial health program for civilian employees. In addition to performing physical examinations on new employees, the staff performed periodic vision and hearing examinations. The dispensary was equipped with a laboratory, an X-ray machine, and electrocardiograph equipment. More severe injuries were transported to the hospital at Mare Island Naval Base. The building was demolished in the 1970s.

Here, Signal Corps members are practicing semaphore around the 1920s.

Seven

World War II

December 7, 1941, was a wet and foggy day in Benicia. Author Josephine Cowell described the scene: "Fog engulfed the arsenal area like thick gray flour shaken from some giant sieve, rendering visibility practically zero and combined with the torn-up condition of post roads and confusion due to the extensive building operations in progress, made difficult the heavy movement of supplies."

Despite the conditions, 125 separate truck convoys were dispatched to installations along the California and Oregon coasts in preparation for an anticipated Japanese invasion. When the final truck left in the early hours of December 8, the arsenal's stock of ammunition, small arms, and high explosives was completely exhausted.

The arsenal became a round-the-clock operation with the acceptance of supplies and raw materials, the manufacture and repair of equipment, and the transshipment of materials to the Pacific Theater or scrap to foundries and factories. The arsenal payroll went from 85 workers in 1940 to 4,535 employees by October 1942.

Women made up 49 percent of the civilian workforce during the war. The link-loading plant was entirely staffed by women, who had a daily output target of linking 500,000 rounds of .30 and .50 caliber ammunition. The plant began operation in May 1942, and by the end of the year, 1,100 women processed 42 billion rounds. (The authors checked this number three times.)

As the war progressed and became more vicious, the number and types of weapons expanded, especially automatic weapons. The types of tracked and wheeled vehicles also expanded, and the arsenal became the point to receive battle-damaged equipment for salvage and rebuilding.

The optical and fire control shop felt the impact of war immediately. Over 14,000 pairs of binoculars were rehabilitated and shipped to the Pacific Theater. The shop also manufactured over 180,000 firing sights for tanks, artillery, and small arms. More than 300 types of instruments from watches to fire control mechanisms were manufactured in the arsenal shops.

In this 1943 photograph, jeeps are being loaded on a freighter. This Army transport was loaded with supplies destined for the Philippines. An infantry detachment of 200 soldiers was ordered to guard the Southern Pacific railroad bridge (shown in the background), an important railroad connection.

Jeeps are being loaded into the freighter in this 1944 photograph. Throughout the war, the arsenal supplied weapons, artillery, parts, and tools. In the first year, Great Britain and North Africa were supplied, but in late 1942, the arsenal was ordered to concentrate on the Pacific.

To support ground troops, 400-gallon potable water tanks mounted on a towing trailer, sometimes called "water buffalos," were shipped along with jeeps to forward areas. These water tanks had an aluminum shell and a stainless-steel inner tank.

This photograph taken in 1943 shows the arsenal receiving bombs shipped in railroad cars from the Midwest. After arrival, they were transferred into Liberty ships for transport to the Pacific theater.

Ammunition handling trucks were used to transport bombs from storage igloos to staging areas for loading onto ships. In most cases, forklift trucks were used in handling pallets of bombs.

Six bombs are loaded using cranes and cables into a Victory ship cargo hold in 1944. The cables are securely affixed to the bombs, despite the haphazard appearance. The officials at the left appear not to be concerned with the process. This photograph also demonstrates the "rolling rings" that were attached to the bombs by the manufacturer to expedite movement. They were removed, and fuses and fins were attached, before loading onto aircraft.

The wharf was the staging area for loading bombs onto ships. Pictured here in 1943 are rows of bombs that have been rolled off the railroad box cars and are awaiting loading onto a Victory ship. Ammunition-handling forklift trucks can be seen as well.

In a ship's cargo hold, arsenal workers carefully pack bombs into shipping containers for safe transport in 1943. The workers communicate with the crane operator to guide the bombs into place. These Victory and Liberty ships could carry 10,000 tons, but usually exceeded that capacity.

Here is another view of two ships along the wharf as 500-pound bombs are moved from a railroad car in January 1945. The shop and storehouse built in 1862 can be seen in the background on the left, and the railroad bridge can be seen on the right.

Tanks were also brought by rail to be shipped to the front lines. Here, new M3 Stuart light tanks are waiting to be loaded onto Liberty ships in about 1944. The buildings in the background are the blacksmith and machine shops built in the 1870s.

Pictured in front of the tank-repair shop in 1943 are two service soldiers in an M22 "Locust" Light Airborne Tank. It was one of the smallest tanks used by the Allies during World War II and was primarily for airborne operations. It was lightweight but was expected to add firepower to airborne forces.

Army officers line up in front of the administration building in 1943. In front is Col. Paul G. Rutten, newly appointed commanding officer. Rutten would command the arsenal throughout World War II.

An LVT-2 Buffalo is seen being inspected in front of the tank shop in 1944. All mechanized vehicles were sent from the arsenal to the theaters of war combat-ready and with their repair and operational kits.

Soldiers stand in formation in front of the enlisted men's quarters (Building 45) in 1943. Soldiers at the arsenal were kept in top physical condition in case they were ordered to front-line duty in Europe or the Pacific. This building is still in use as private apartments.

This view of the inside of the enlisted men's barracks quarters shows rows of bunks, lockers, and uniforms in 1943. The soldier in the photograph is Cpl. J.A. Wyse. The quarters were compact, as there were only three feet between bunks and few windows. Each soldier had a footlocker to store his belongings.

Women worked in crowded conditions in a leather shop upstairs in Building 57, which was erected in 1884. They are using Singer industrial sewing machines. The electrical power was fed from the ceiling, and motors were controlled by foot pedals underneath the workstations. Large windows can be seen in the background. A poster advertising the seventh war bond campaign reveals the date as 1945.

Nica Jordan (left) and Alice Boyle are assembling recoil mechanisms for .50 caliber anti-aircraft guns. Jordan was a five-year veteran at the arsenal, having formerly worked in the canvas, leather, and small arms shops. Alice's husband, William, was a rigger at the Mare Island Naval Shipyard.

Small ammunition was received packaged in crates with bullets in boxes of 10 in 1943. Here, women workers are unpacking the ammunition so that it could be placed in a belting machine. The civilian workforce was racially integrated during the war, but the women reported that they preferred to work with no men around.

These women are working on ammunition belting in 1943. Bullets were manually placed into a machine that assembled them into belts of about 200 rounds. Every fifth round was usually a tracer so the gunner could follow their track at night. Hard hats and safety equipment did not become available in women's sizes until later in the war, so women were often photographed wearing oversized men's equipment.

Two women are inspecting the belted ammunition. Note the improvised safety gloves that are too large for them, and the lack of hard hats or protective work clothes.

Elizabeth Tucker (left) and Ruth Vollmers, munitions inspectors at the arsenal, give final inspection to 90 mm anti-aircraft shells in 1944. They are preparing the ammunition for firing in the cannon test tunnels.

Taken in 1944, this photograph shows Jessie Larson welding a Sherman tank turret in the tank shop. Several of the women workers were students who went to Benicia High School in the morning and worked at the arsenal or at the adjacent Yuba Manufacturing Company in the afternoon. Decades later, Larson returned with her grandchildren to show them where she fought the war.

Sherman tanks are seen lined up in the service area in front of the tank shop in 1944. The building on the left is now a self-storage facility and the building on the right houses a wallpaper factory.

This is T.Sgt. (T/5) Robert Carr of the Port Company Detail. Technical sergeants had unique skills but were not trained as combat leaders. Those who held the rank of T/5 were addressed as "corporal," the same as the corresponding noncommissioned officer at the same pay grade. Technical Sergeant Carr was probably an inspector.

Rifles were routinely repaired, aligned, and reconditioned. Here, an arsenal worker is cleaning rifle bores, 10 at a time. After combat, soldiers and Marines exchanged their weapons for new ones and the used weapons were returned for reconditioning or scrap.

A service expert is photographed conducting an examination of a 155 mm howitzer tube. During this era, the Army allowed soldiers to name their tanks and cannons and paint the name and artwork on the gun tube. This tube, named "Belching Babe," shows evidence of having been in combat.

Tons of chemical warfare agents such as mustard gas, sarin, and tabun were stockpiled at the arsenal to be used against Japan. They were stored in special igloos in the eastern part of the arsenal. With the chemical agents came the need to decontaminate soldiers who may have been accidentally exposed. This photograph, taken in 1944, shows a decontamination shower.

Taken in 1944, this photograph shows part of the chemical warfare decontamination equipment. Soaping was necessary to break up any chemical agent that may have contacted a worker, especially mustard agents that were thick and tenacious.

This 1944 photograph shows the decontamination equipment in operation. Decontamination showers removed the spilled or over-sprayed chemical agents. This equipment could also be used for the removal of industrial solvents.

Pictured in 1944, the arsenal had a small fleet of tugboats for moving barges and ships. The smaller tugs were called "Little Toots" and were manufactured by the Le-Boeuf-Dougherty Company of Richmond, California. These tugs saved the government $40,000 per year by not contracting civilian tugboats.

Shown in 1944, LVTs (landing vehicles tracked) are loaded on barges at the arsenal wharf. Behind them, two Victory ships are moored. The LVTs were barged to Hunters Point Naval Shipyard to be loaded onto assault ships.

This aerial photograph taken in 1944 shows the Southern Pacific railroad right of way running through the eastern part of the arsenal. Just above center are the igloos that the chemical warfare agents were stored in. The warehouses in the background and foreground are still in use.

Yuba Manufacturing Co., adjacent to the arsenal, manufactured most of the artillery used by the US forces in World War II. This photograph taken in 1943 shows artillery barrels during manufacture at the main Yuba plant.

Vehicles are lined up at the main gate for a parade in 1945. This was a victory parade to show off the equipment the arsenal had been working on for the previous three and a half years. The parking lot on the right and the apartments on the left are now replaced by townhouses. The Spanish revival headquarters building is behind and to the left of the vehicles.

Another service area is pictured here, with Sherman tanks and trailers awaiting evaluation and repair in 1944. The volume of work on equipment returned from the combat theaters was tremendous and there was no time to keep the work areas neat and tidy. Weapons and body parts were sometimes found in vehicles returned from combat.

Army tugboats were also used to transfer barges of military equipment to the Army base at Oakland, California. Oakland built a huge waterfront terminal and began performing its military mission in 1944 as a transportation port and distribution terminal.

The *Army Queen* is pictured at the Benicia Army Wharf in 1945. A converted civilian ship, the *Queen* sailed the waters of the San Francisco Bay and the California Delta connecting Army and Navy installations.

Army personnel at the arsenal draw books from a library on wheels, which visited the arsenal on alternate weeks. It was the only library of its kind in the Army and was run by the 9th Service Command Unit, which serviced posts throughout Northern California.

These M1A1 75mm pack howitzers were returned from use or withheld from shipment and stored outdoors in about 1945. The weapon, with a range of 9,600 yards, was mounted on a conventional M8 airborne carriage to serve as a field artillery piece. These howitzers met the need for an artillery piece that was transportable across difficult terrain and could be broken down into pieces to be carried by pack animals.

Equipment was stored in vast parking lots in preparation for transshipment to the Pacific Theater. The chemical warfare agent storage igloos can be seen at left. They were destroyed in 1954 when all the agents were shipped to Utah. The Carquinez Strait is in the background, and there are not yet any mothballed ships. The area to the right is now the Valero refinery.

Amphibious LVTs were stored at the arsenal in 1945. The tree-lined road is all that remained of the Benicia Barracks that were built in the 1850s and destroyed in the 1922 fire. At the end of the war, every square foot of terrain at the arsenal was covered with parked vehicles either stopped in shipment or returned from the theaters of war.

In 1944, the US Army Service Corps offered Italian POWs the opportunity to join Italian Service Units. The volunteers were given jobs, monetary compensation, and freedom of movement. Italian men are shown here building their barracks. Behind the new barracks are the tents that initially housed them.

This image shows the Italian Service Unit constructing a dining hall in 1944. Wood was scarce, so the men re-used surplus wooden shipping crates.

The Italian Service Unit built this assembly hall from wooden crates in 1944. The Italian dance band is posing in the rear left side of the hall.

The Italians relaxed in their free time by playing bocce ball on a court that they constructed, as seen here in 1944.

The Italians had their own mess hall where spaghetti was served in 1944. The Italian Service Unit was limited in its assignments. They could not handle munitions or weapons but were busy recycling metals and wood and building structures such as sidewalks. Many of the sidewalks they constructed are still used in the eastern part of Benicia.

The California Youth Authority sent volunteer wards to help at the arsenal, and the Italian Service Unit worked side-by-side with them on projects. Here, they are building a stone wall just inside the arsenal's main gate in 1944. The house is gone but the wall still exists.

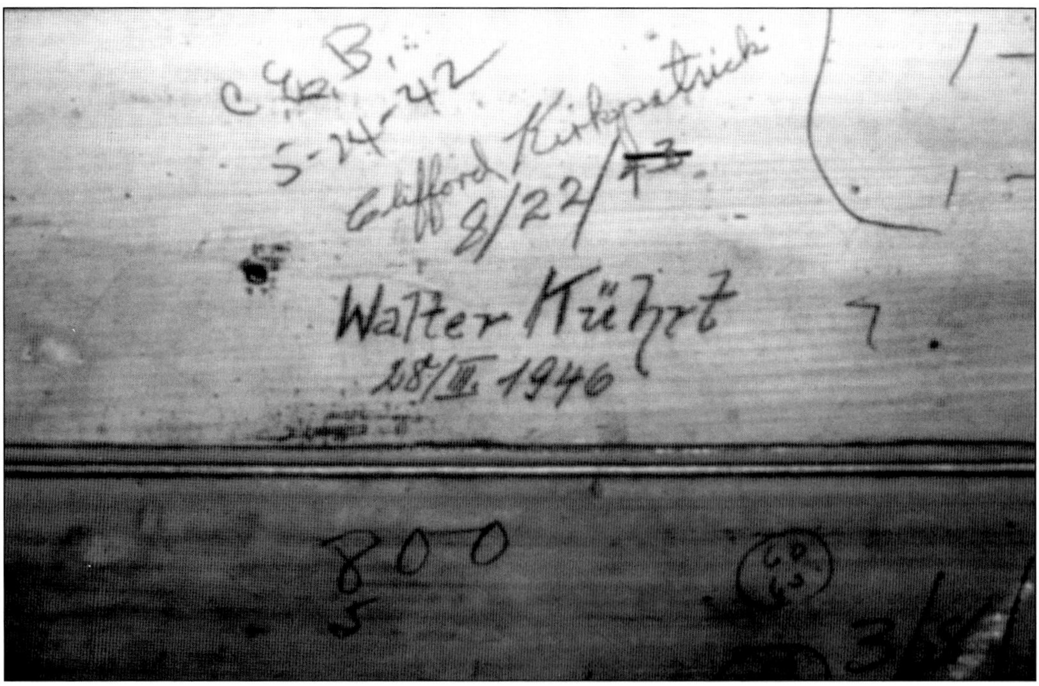

While the Italians were happy to be at the arsenal, the German POWs were not. German POW Corporal Walter Kührt was captured on August 15, 1944, in France and was in camps in California before being transferred to Benicia. He inscribed his name and date on the wall inside Powder Magazine 10 on March 28, 1946. It took over two years to repatriate all POWs to Italy, Germany, and Japan. (Allan Gandy.)

The funeral procession for German POW Alfred Stark is pictured here. Stark died November 21, 1945, at the arsenal and was buried at the Benicia Army Cemetery. The procession consisted of US Army personnel and German POWs. In June 1946, the former prisoners were transferred to the port of San Francisco for embarkation back to Germany.

This is a modern photograph of German POW graves. From left to right are (first row) Ernst Gall; (second row) Willi Behrens, Heinz Knoph, Werner Mattner, Hans Fischer, Alfred Stark, Karl Hafer, and Richard Neuhaus.

Boy Scouts from Benicia Troop 1 are seen sorting newspapers after a paper drive around 1945. The Scouts participated in flag ceremonies, service projects, and other similar events. They were never allowed to handle munitions or weapons.

Sherman tanks are parked waiting for the next war, about 1946. The arsenal received hundreds of Sherman tanks after the war for reconditioning and storage. This image shows the tanks in an outside storage area on the arsenal grounds. Pictured in the distance is the US Navy "mothball fleet" anchored in Suisun Bay.

Eight

Korea, the Cold War, NATO, and SEATO

Up until V-J Day, the arsenal was going at full steam to win the war. Plans were in place to invade Japan, and the armed forces needed the implements of war. The arsenal was in the process of shipping west tons of chemical warfare agents. All this came to a halt after the Japanese surrender. Thousands of pieces of equipment had to be returned to the arsenal and prepared for storage, scrapping, or reuse. Hundreds of tons of ammunition were found to be obsolete or damaged and were destroyed in gigantic burning pits and cages.

The arsenal still had to support armies of occupation in Europe and Japan and the troops tasked with searching the battlefields for bodies, mines, and unexploded ordnance. The civilian personnel strength gradually declined to 1,402 employees and then climbed to 2,389 as the United States engaged in Mutual Defense Assistance Pact programs such as NATO and SEATO.

When the Korean War started on June 25, 1953, the process of reactivation was not as dramatic as it was nine years earlier after the Pearl Harbor attack. The number of employees increased from 2,274 to 6,712. Hundreds of tons of equipment and supplies were transshipped to the Korean peninsula.

In the decade following the end of the Korean War, the rollback of the material of war resumed. There was still equipment from World War II to sort through, and the Korean War added to the burden. Equipment still needed to be provided to SEATO forces, including Vietnam, and to Korea to maintain the US Army presence there and to equip the Republic of Korea forces.

The resultant rollbacks created massive stocks of supplies spread out in Army depots throughout California. For example, three complete field hospitals were sitting in crates in the arsenal. The result was surplus sales often selling equipment to private companies for pennies on the dollar. In 1954, the arsenal placed $3,779,106 worth of equipment on sale, which sold for $342,245.

In 1954, guided missiles made their appearance at the arsenal, which became the logistics base for Nike, Nike Hercules, and Corporal missiles in the San Francisco Bay area. Shown here is the administrative building proudly displaying Nike missiles. Today, the missiles are gone, and the building is full of offices.

Two officers stand by a sign for C Battery, 9th Artillery Battalion, orderly room in front of the battery headquarters. The "AA" in the shield symbol stands for anti-aircraft, specifically Nike missiles.

Silhouetted against a cloudy sky, a Nike missile at the arsenal makes an impressive picture as Capt. Edward W. Nicholls, Battery B, 740th AAA Missile Battalion commanding officer (right), talks with 1st Lt. Arthur C. Shepard (center) and M.Sgt. Thomas K. Crawford.

Men of Battery B, 740th AAA Missile Battalion deal with duties at a tracking radar of a mobile Nike installation at the arsenal. At the telescope is Pfc. Donald L. Kidder, and on the ground from left to right are M.Sgt. Harold R. Myers, Sgt. William Punt Jr, and Sfc. Leonard C. Crenshaw.

An Army chaplain provides a Sunday prayer service to a group of soldiers in a field at the arsenal. These soldiers supported the upgrade and testing of Nike missiles. Two missiles can be seen in the background. Note the portable altar and organ.

Nike missile crews uncrate, assemble, and test missiles in 1955. Missile assembly consisted of the installation of the control fins, main fins, ailerons, and fairings. The hydraulic and propulsion systems were also checked. Special carts provided ease of servicing and moving the missiles.

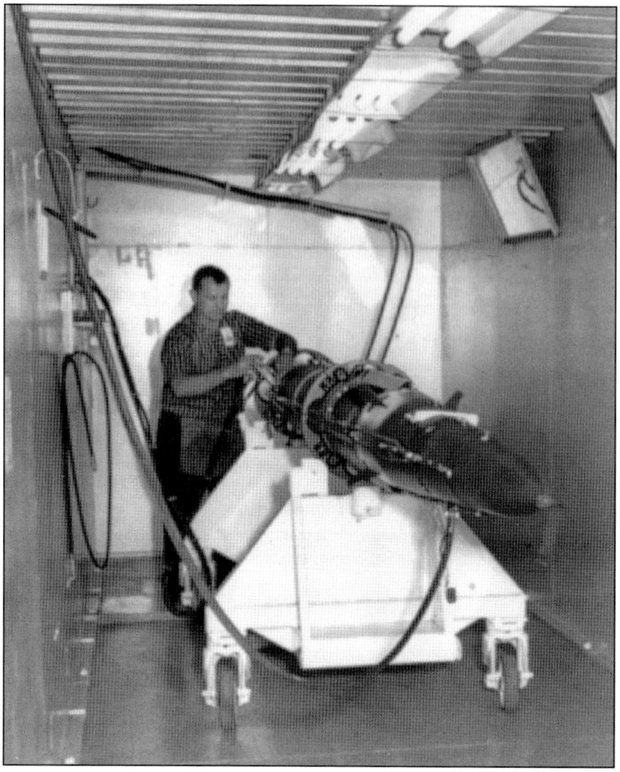

A Nike Ajax missile is being serviced in a special "acid" room in 1955. The missile used a solid propellant booster and liquid propellant second stage. The liquid sustainer engine produced 2,600 pounds of thrust for about 20 seconds by using highly toxic red-fuming nitric acid and jet fuel as its propellants.

The arsenal had a facility for decontamination because the missile fuel was so toxic. The fuel mixture was the most dangerous substance ever kept on the arsenal grounds.

Nike missiles were stored in special containers in warehouses known as Storage Transitory Shelters. The buildings were designed with a high roof and minimal columns to accommodate the storage of large pieces of equipment.

Unused Army supplies were returned to the arsenal from the Pacific Theater of Operations for reuse or disposal, as pictured in 1955. It took over a decade to return used and unused supplies and equipment to the United States. These workers are doing the tedious task of sorting through boxes of supplies. Most of the Army surplus was auctioned at pennies on the dollar.

This view shows the arsenal lands on the Carquinez Straits in the 1950s. The mothball fleet is anchored in the background, and the crescent of land between the railroad and the water is infilled from hydraulic mining in the Sierra Nevada mountains during the Gold Rush. To the left is Sulphur Springs Creek, and to the right of it is the burn yard, the most contaminated part of the facility.

Most of the returned materials were stored outdoors on vast hardstands in the same condition they were received, for example, in crates unprotected from the weather. The equipment for three entire field hospitals, infantry divisions, airfields, and maintenance facilities was either stopped en route to the Pacific theater or returned.

This photograph shows the arsenal fire station in the 1950s. The station was built during World War II and replaced the brick and stone facility built in 1872. It is now used as a vehicle repair garage.

Laid down late in the war, the Victory ship *Sgt. Andrew Miller* is tied up at the arsenal wharf in 1948. Even though the war was over, the arsenal was busy receiving used and unused equipment and sorting through it for transshipment to China and Europe. The Cold War exploded right after World War II and kept the arsenal busy for another decade.

Unusable military small arms and munitions were returned following the Korean War. The destruction and burning area in a ravine at the arsenal is seen here, with a large container of dangerous items being destroyed. The Army conducted a large-scale cleanup of the area, but unfortunately, they did not get it all, thus creating a problem that would remain unsettled 67 years later.

Gen. Hwang Yup of the Republic of Korea visited the arsenal in June 1954 on the final stop of a tour of the United States, during which he consulted with military leaders in Washington and visited numerous Army installations. General Yup was greeted by Lt. Col. Daniel W. Allison, arsenal commanding officer, and Capt. Haston R. Zablackas, interpreter and tour director.

Shown here in 1954 is a row of Japanese American women filing cards in a warehouse. They were employed as editors in the availability edit section of the 229th Ordnance Company in 1955.

Taken in the 1950s, this photograph shows the railroad network, called the "Christmas Tree" by the civilian workforce. Mt. Diablo is in the far-right background and the mothball fleet is in the left background. The igloos for the chemical weapons are in the upper mid background. In the foreground are shops for Nike missile maintenance.

The Army occasionally recognized civilian employees for their contributions. Here are seven men and two women receiving certificates for their performance in 1955.

The Benicia Arsenal Employees Association published the *Benicia Arsenal Magazine* from 1951 to 1953. In this issue from March 1951, "The Post Restaurant is Big Business" tells the story of how the arsenal restaurant was feeding 6,200 people daily.

The arsenal had two modern cafeterias, one in the administrative area and one in warehouse W-9. They served breakfast and noon meals at nominal prices. Pictured here is the cafeteria when it opened in 1953.

The arsenal telephone system had a switchboard connected to the Pacific Telephone Company. Two internal radio networks were maintained, one for the civilian police force and the other for the motor pool.

Teletype facilities were in the headquarters building and were part of the Army network to receive and transmit messages around the world. Western Union telegraph services for government and civilian personnel were also in the teletype office.

In the 1950s, a Military Affiliate Radio System station was in Building 8, staffed by civilians during off-duty hours to provide amateur radio communications to military people across the globe. Personnel trained on their own time to be available to respond to a disaster. This building is now the office of the Benicia Historical Museum.

Josephine Williams Cowell worked at the Stockton Arsenal as a historian for four years during World War II. Prior to her service with the Ordnance Corps, Cowell was a student at the University of California and acquired credits at the College of the Pacific in Stockton. After graduation, she worked for the *Stockton Record* for 11 years and the *Stockton Morning Independent* for 4 years. In February 1953, Cowell was appointed the official arsenal historian as a public information officer.

Cowell authored a book titled *History of Benicia Arsenal, Benicia, California*, published in 1963. After the closure of the arsenal in 1964, she worked at the Tooele Army Depot in Utah until retiring in March 1967. She is shown here at her farewell party receiving congratulations from an Army officer in 1964.

Nine

Conversion into Benicia Industrial Park

On March 30, 1961, the Benicia Arsenal received a teletype message from the Army Chief of Ordnance that stunned the installation personnel. It read, "Benicia Arsenal, Benicia, California will be inactivated by closeout and/or transfer of mission." The date of the inactivation was set for March 30, 1964.

The procedure at the time for base closure was to turn the property over to the General Services Administration once it was declared surplus. In turn, the GSA planned to apply to the arsenal its usual three options of property disposal: transfer the property to another federal agency, sell it to another government entity such as a state university, or divide it into small lots and sell them to private entities by auction.

One of the federal agencies interested in the property was NASA, and Benicia became one of the three finalists for the Manned Spacecraft Center, which was eventually located in Houston.

The impact of the closing was apparent to the residents of Benicia, and the community response was immediate. Mayor James Lemos called an emergency meeting the evening of the announcement. A "Save the Arsenal" movement was launched, and a committee was organized. The conversion of the Benicia Arsenal into the Benicia Industrial Park was the brainchild of two men: John Bohn, the city attorney who provided legal expertise and guidance, and James Lemos, the mayor, who provided political leadership.

The process of closing the arsenal and transferring ownership to the City of Benicia took 20 years and involved an act of Congress, four acts of the California legislature, four new laws, five deeds, four leases, a survey, two appraisals, multiple meetings, two US presidents, two state governors, an assortment of senators, Congress members, legislators, at least four federal agencies, and one lawsuit won by the city. The deed for the arsenal from the US government to the City of Benicia was signed in February 1965. Today, the former arsenal is a 2,900-acre industrial park hosting 300 businesses, including a refinery and the Benicia Historical Museum.

RATE INCREASE
TION FOR SCHOOLS
DAY, APRIL 4

THE BENICIAN

BENICIA'S ONLY HOME-OWNED NEWSPAPER

Volume Fourteen — Number Thirty-five

Benicia, Solano County, California, Friday, March 31, 1961

Defense Department Orders Benicia Arsenal Inactivated In 3 Years

A teletype from the Secretary of Defense to Col. Albert C. Wells, Jr., commanding officer of Benicia Arsenal stated that Benicia Arsenal was to be inactivated during the next three years and then closed.

Benicia Arsenal was one of four ordnance installation's ordered inactivated and closed-out. One other, Redstone Arsenal, in Alabama, was ordered transferred to the U. S. Army Missile department.

The message shocked the residents of Benicia and Solano County. The Arsenal is the largest of the installations ordered inactivated and closed-out. The others included Mt. Rainier, Tacoma, Washington; Raritan in New Jersey and Rosslord in Toledo, Ohio.

The announcement was made at an 8:15 hurriedly called press meeting at Benicia Arsenal.

The teletype follows:
Department of Defense,
Washington, D. C.
To Commanding Officer,
Benicia Arsenal.

The Secretary of Defense is making an announcement at 1000 hours, EST, 30 March 1961 concerning the inactivation of four ordnance depots and 1 depot activity.

Inactivation of the following installations over a three year period follows:

Benicia Arsenal, Benicia, California, will be inactivated by close-out or transfer of mission to

Cong. John Baldwin Protests Arsenal Action

Editor, The Benician,
Benicia, Calif.

Congressman John F. Baldwin (R) of California this morning released the following telegram which he has just dispatched to President Kennedy relative to the proposed inactivation of Benicia Arsenal announced by the Defense Department:

"I have today received notice from the Defense Department that Benicia Arsenal, at Benicia, California, is to be inactivated and closed over a three year period.

"Since the Defense Department is under instructions that no public announcements are to be made unless authorized by the administration, it is evident that this decision has been made with your knowledge and approval. I should

Mayor James Lemos Calls Emergency Meeting

Mayor James Lemos has called an emergency meeting of organizations and citizens for this evening (Thursday).

The meeting will start at eight o'clock in the council chambers.

Among the organizations to be represented are: the Armed Serv-

EGG HUNT NDAY – IF IT RAIN

Highland Residents Protest Apartment Buildings

This 1961 newspaper article announces the arsenal closure. The news set off a series of actions that were first aimed at preventing the closure of the arsenal and, when that effort failed, to turn it into a business park.

A military parade was held for the final retreat of the colors and the closing of the arsenal in March 1964. A military parade is not a show of force but is ceremonial since movement is restricted by close-order maneuvering and marching. The soldiers shown here are in dress uniforms with rifles, and the color guard is present. Boy Scouts stand at attention along the side of the road.

In this scene on the parade ground in front of the administration building in 1964, soldiers are folding the flag after it was lowered for the last time. A plaque was later erected by Benicia Parlor No. 89, Native Sons of the Golden West, dedicating the arsenal as California Historical Landmark No. 176.

This is an aerial view of the arsenal before its closing in 1953. It covered 2,900 acres and consisted of 191 permanent structures, 91 semipermanent structures, and 40 temporary buildings. The cost of government-owned assets (land, buildings, and equipment) was $39,858,433. The US government sold the arsenal to the City of Benicia for $4.5 million.

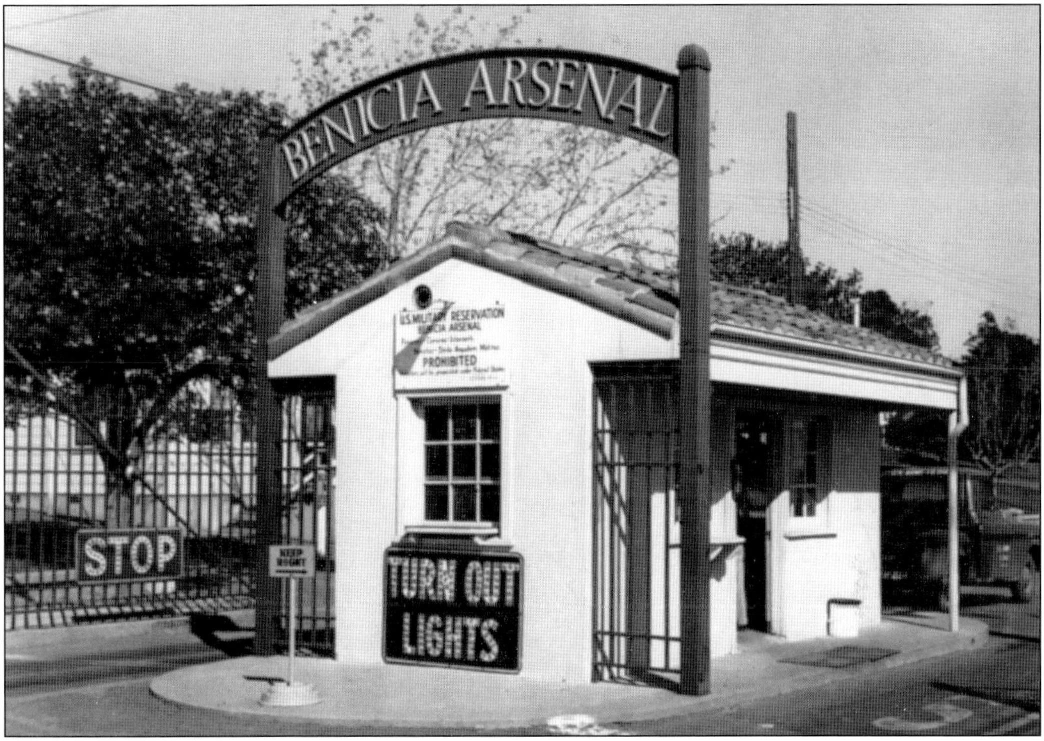

The main gate to the arsenal is seen here at the time of closing. Today, the building is gone but the gates remain, welded permanently back to allow unrestricted traffic.

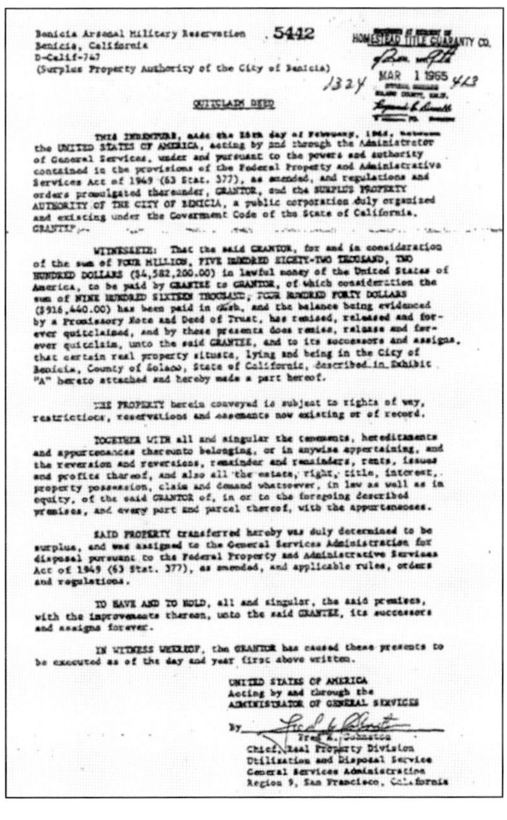

Benicia Arsenal Military Reservation 5442
Benicia, California
D-Calif-747
(Surplus Property Authority of the City of Benicia)

HOMESTEAD TITLE GUARANTY CO.
MAR 1 1965

QUITCLAIM DEED

THIS INDENTURE, made the [illegible] day of February, 1965, between the UNITED STATES OF AMERICA, acting by and through the Administrator of General Services, under and pursuant to the powers and authority contained in the provisions of the Federal Property and Administrative Services Act of 1949 (63 Stat. 377), as amended, and regulations and orders promulgated thereunder, GRANTOR, and the SURPLUS PROPERTY AUTHORITY OF THE CITY OF BENICIA, a public corporation duly organized and existing under the Government Code of the State of California, GRANTEE.

WITNESSETH: That the said GRANTOR, for and in consideration of the sum of FOUR MILLION, FIVE HUNDRED EIGHTY-TWO THOUSAND, TWO HUNDRED DOLLARS ($4,582,200.00) in lawful money of the United States of America, to be paid by GRANTEE to GRANTOR, of which consideration the sum of NINE HUNDRED SIXTEEN THOUSAND, FOUR HUNDRED FORTY DOLLARS ($916,440.00) has been paid in cash, and the balance being evidenced by a Promissory Note and Deed of Trust, has remised, released and forever quitclaimed, and by these presents does remise, release and forever quitclaim, unto the said GRANTEE, and to its successors and assigns, that certain real property situate, lying and being in the City of Benicia, County of Solano, State of California, described in Exhibit "A" hereto attached and hereby made a part hereof.

THE PROPERTY herein conveyed is subject to rights of way, restrictions, reservations and easements now existing or of record.

TOGETHER WITH all and singular the tenements, hereditaments and appurtenances thereunto belonging, or in anywise appertaining, and the reversion and reversions, remainder and remainders, rents, issues and profits thereof, and also all the estate, right, title, interest, property possession, claim and demand whatsoever, in law as well as in equity, of the said GRANTOR of, in or to the foregoing described premises, and every part and parcel thereof, with the appurtenances.

SAID PROPERTY transferred hereby was duly determined to be surplus, and was assigned to the General Services Administration for disposal pursuant to the Federal Property and Administrative Services Act of 1949 (63 Stat. 377), as amended, and applicable rules, orders and regulations.

TO HAVE AND TO HOLD, all and singular, the said premises, with the improvements thereon, unto the said GRANTEE, its successors and assigns forever.

IN WITNESS WHEREOF, the GRANTOR has caused these presents to be executed as of the day and year first above written.

UNITED STATES OF AMERICA
Acting by and through the
ADMINISTRATOR OF GENERAL SERVICES

By ____________
Fred A. Johnston
Chief, Real Property Division
Utilization and Disposal Service
General Services Administration
Region 9, San Francisco, California

The United States deeded the arsenal to the City of Benicia for $4.5 million. There were five deeds in all, plus the deeds for the water, road, electricity, railroad, and telephone systems.

The official ground breaking of the Benicia Industrial Park (BIP) occurred in 1964. Shown from left to right are Michael Fitzgerald, city council member; Marvin Kenny, city manager; David Stringfellow, president of Benicia Industries; Warren O'Blennis, city council member; James Lemos, mayor of Benicia; Zeck Moreira; John Bohm, city attorney; and unidentified. The BIP encompasses over seven million square feet of floor space on 2,900 acres, housing over 300 businesses that employ more than 7,000 people, representing 50 percent of Benicia's total private employment. The largest industrial park in Solano County, the BIP includes a wide variety of business types, including manufacturing, construction, environmental engineering, steel fabrication, petroleum refining, logistics, distribution, warehousing, biotech, and port operations.

Arthur Stern Architectural Glass was one of the first companies to occupy the deserted arsenal buildings after the closing. The company is still operational, and its creations are featured in buildings around the world. (James Lessenger.)

Many of the businesses in Benicia Industrial Park represent small business owners. Pictured is Brad Adams, a woodturner, in his single-suite unit in an industrial building. Since 2006, Adams has specialized in wood bowls, vases, and vessels. He uses a variety of wood burls including maple, Tasmanian blackwood, madrone, oak, walnut, myrtle, camphor, and pecan. (Allan Gandy.)

This photograph taken in 2022 shows the former carpentry shop. Since its construction in the 1880s, it has gone through multiple changes and is now artists' studios on the ground floor and the Bradbury and Bradbury vintage wallpaper plant on the top floor. (Allan Gandy.)

One of the first major companies to open in Benicia after the arsenal closure was the Humble Oil Company. Humble broke ground for its new refinery in 1966 and came online in 1969. At that time, it was the most modern and efficient refinery in the nation, utilizing the latest technology to convert a variety of crude oils into finished petroleum products, primarily gasoline, jet fuels, and diesel. Over the decades, the ownership of the refinery has gone from Humble to Exxon to Valero, which now runs it.

The Benicia National Guard Amory is the home of the California National Guard's 749 Combat Sustainment Battalion. The armory was constructed on land purchased by the city from the US government and then gifted to the Guard. (James Lessenger.)

The commanding officers' quarters is seen in the 1950s. It was the Commandant's Residence restaurant in the 1980s until closed by 14 health department violations. It is now fully restored by the City of Benicia and is an art gallery and educational center operated by Arts Benicia.

This is one of the 109 munitions bunkers built on the arsenal in the three years prior to World War II. Today, it is used as a paint storage locker for the California Department of Transportation (Caltrans). (James Lessenger.)

Built just before World War II, these were small arms ammunition facilities where the belting assembly lines were located. Today, they house Dunlop Manufacturing, a company that manufactures electronic musical equipment. (James Lessenger.)

The Benicia Historical Museum opened in 1985 and occupies Building 9 of the old "camel barn" complex. The buildings are owned by the City of Benicia and leased to a non-profit museum corporation. The top floor of Building 9 is a display space, and the bottom floor is a large event room. (James Lessenger.)

In this photograph taken in 2022, the Valero Refinery is shown, with part of the industrial park and the mothball fleet behind it. The vegetation is kept trimmed by using goats. The Carquinez Strait and the foothills of Mt. Diablo are in the background.

Taken in 2022, this is a photograph of the ironworkers training center. To the right and out of the camera view is the union hall. Appropriately, these facilities are across the street from the refinery and near four bridges that span the Carquinez Strait. (Allan Gandy.)

This is a modern photograph of the Bradbury and Bradbury wallpaper manufacturing company. Using a silk screen process and sophisticated inks, the company recreates 19th century wallpaper designs that are used across the world. This room is in the former leather equipment manufacturing building, the center of the three buildings seen on page 41. It is also the same room seen in use during World War II on page 76. (Allan Gandy.)

Taken in 2022, this image is of the interior of the same arsenal building used for tank repair that is shown on the cover of this book and in chapter seven. It is still in use today as a machine shop run by the Unico Mechanical Corporation. This photograph shows work being done on components of the California Water Project, the largest water delivery project in the world. (Allan Gandy.)

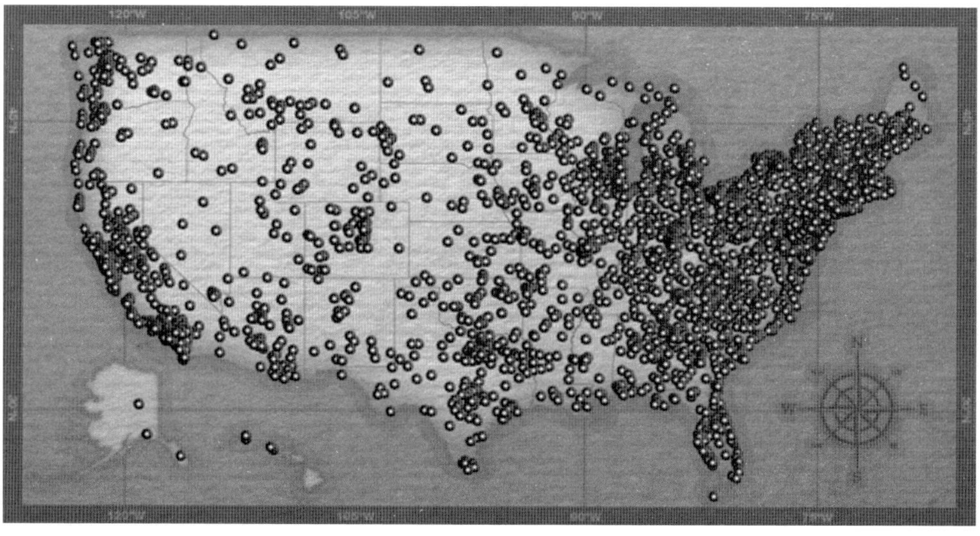

Consistent with our mission to preserve history on a local level, this book was printed in South Carolina on American-made paper and manufactured entirely in the United States. Products carrying the accredited Forest Stewardship Council (FSC) label are printed on 100 percent FSC-certified paper.

MADE IN THE USA